INTRODUCTION TO
RESEARCH IN AMERICAN HISTORY

THE MACMILLAN COMPANY
NEW YORK · BOSTON · CHICAGO · DALLAS
ATLANTA · SAN FRANCISCO

MACMILLAN & CO., LIMITED
LONDON · BOMBAY · CALCUTTA
MELBOURNE

THE MACMILLAN COMPANY
OF CANADA, LIMITED
TORONTO

INTRODUCTION
TO
RESEARCH IN AMERICAN HISTORY

BY

HOMER CAREY HOCKETT

PROFESSOR OF HISTORY IN
THE OHIO STATE UNIVERSITY

New York
THE MACMILLAN COMPANY

Set up and printed.
Published May, 1931.

Seventh printing April, 1942.

SET UP, ELECTROTYPED, AND PRINTED BY T. MOREY & SON

IN THE UNITED STATES OF AMERICA

PREFACE

Any university teacher who supervises the first efforts of graduate students to produce historical compositions soon wearies of the endless repetition of substantially identical directions. In the effort to transfer this burden from teacher to textbook, several excellent manuals have been written during the last few years. Some of these discuss the methods employed in educational research as well as in the social sciences; others discuss the techniques of all the social sciences, of which history is but one. Still others which treat of history only are extremely brief and compact, leaving much explanatory comment to be supplied by the instructor. Moreover, in those instances where the authors are not themselves workers in the historical field, there is usually some deviation, in the forms given for bibliographies and footnotes, from the practice of historians.

The experience of the present writer seems to point to the need of a guide for the beginner in historical research and writing, in which nothing but the essential procedures in this field are dealt with. These procedures present enough difficulties even when not complicated by the discussion of related techniques. For similar reasons the presentation of historical method herein is limited to the American field, a plan which it is believed affords the maximum opportunity for concentration on essentials, a thorough grounding in which is most readily attainable when they are divorced so far as may be from all collateral considerations. This manual attempts to make the path so plain that a student of capacity sufficient to earn an advanced degree may proceed with little more guidance than it affords. It has therefore seemed wise to take nothing for granted, even at the risk of stressing the obvious.

For the student who possesses a working knowledge of the

v

appropriate foreign languages, this manual may serve as an introduction to the field of European historical research, if the instructor will contribute the appropriate supplementary list of aids for finding the materials for that field. With such an introduction to procedures as this book attempts to provide, the acquisition of a working knowledge of these additional tools should be a comparatively simple matter.

HOMER CAREY HOCKETT

THE OHIO STATE UNIVERSITY
    April, 1931

TABLE OF CONTENTS

INTRODUCTION

There are many definitions of history, but it is perhaps sufficient to say that the term denotes any effort to recount or describe any portion or phase of the past life of humankind. History may treat of war, diplomacy, art, institutions, travel, science, industry, biography, or thought. All of these, or any of them, or any part of one or more of them, is suitable subject-matter. The potential range of the historian is as wide as life itself.

A thoughtless person might suppose that the writing of history is a simple matter, a mere gathering of facts and putting them together in a connected way. But neither the gathering of facts nor the putting them together is a very easy process. It is true that even a child of normal capacity may be taught to collect simple data from a number of sources and to combine them in an original form; but in their advanced aspects both collection and presentation require superior mentality and special training. Moreover, between the collecting of material and its composition into a finished account a third process, known as criticism, must intervene.

There are, then, three essential processes in the art of producing history: the gathering of data, the criticism of data, and the presentation of facts in a readable form. While these steps are not necessarily taken separately in practice, they require separate discussion, since they are logically distinct and each has its own technique. The purpose of this manual is to explain these techniques.

The gathering of data pertinent to any subject which one may undertake to investigate requires a considerable technical equipment. This is true even if all of the material is available in printed form, and in the English language. Many researches involve the examination of documents in German, French, or other foreign languages; the reading of medieval Latin chronicles; or even the deciphering of ancient Roman or Greek monuments, Egyptian hieroglyphics, or Assyrian tablets. The requisite linguistic equipment varies, of course, with the field in which the investigation falls; so does the knowledge which may be required of such "auxiliary sciences" as epigraphy, paleography, and diplomatics.

The auxiliary sciences, however indispensable they may be for work in some fields of history, are aids or tools employed by the historian when occasion requires, rather than essential parts of his procedure. This is not true of the three processes mentioned in the preceding paragraphs, for any bit of investigation which eventuates in a written product involves all three of them. They can therefore be presented most simply and lucidly if dissociated at first from the study of the auxiliaries.

The process of collecting data does not yield material in form for use in historical composition. Such material is in the raw, and cannot be safely utilized until it has been subjected to critical examination. It is the principles of criticism which are most commonly meant when the term "historical science" is used. These principles require careful study. Yet there is no part of the historian's task which the beginner is so prone to slight as the critical examination of his data. He must learn to combat the natural tendency to credulity, and to cultivate an attitude of scepticism. He needs to realize, at the outset, that his material is in large part made up of statements of more or less partisan, ignorant, unscrupulous, careless, or incompetent persons. The principles by which such statements are tested and sifted are in reality nothing more than common-sense rules carefully formulated, but a thoughtful study of this branch of procedure will help in avoiding blunders which are inevitable if one learns one's lessons merely from one's own unguided efforts and experiences.

The culminating effort of the historian, for which everything else is preparatory, is of course the synthesis of the sifted data into an accurate and readable account of the matter investigated. It is to the finished product that others will look for evidence that the undertaking has been worth while. Many difficulties beset the writer in this stage of his labors. In the first place, his "eye must be single." Even though he cannot hope to tell the whole truth, he must strive to tell nothing but the truth. With the most honest intentions, he will find it difficult to be impartial, because of his own preconceptions, or party, sectarian, racial, national, or other group associations and consequent bias. Indeed, it is not given to man to escape bias of some kind altogether.

When the writer has done his best in this regard, there is still a technique of presentation to which he must conform. That is to say, in order to be professionally orthodox, a historical production must include bibliographies and footnotes, drawn up in the form prescribed by recognized usage. Finally the effectiveness of the production will be proportionate to the skill with which the writer can use the English language.

In addition to the techniques of the three processes discussed in this manual, there is a certain minimum of preparation which is presupposed in the case of one who undertakes even a modest contribution to historical literature. The curriculum of a standard College of Liberal Arts provides an adequate general education, and an undergraduate major in the social sciences should yield a sufficient acquaintance with subject-matter and point of view in the historical field. If the writer is a graduate student in a university, he should pursue one or more "background" courses during the first year of graduate study, in order to give solidity and breadth of information in the particular field in which the thesis falls. One who is working independently must make up for the lack of such courses by extensive reading.

Besides all this, the person who attacks a historical theme should have learned certain fundamental lessons from his earlier studies. From the natural sciences he should have gained some insight into the scientific method—the functions of observation, experiment, and hypothesis in the reasoning process, and the relations of cause and effect; from biology and the social sciences he should have learned that there is a continuity in life which runs through all changes, and that this principle of continuity obtains in the history of human institutions and relationships; from linguistic studies he should have gained the power to express his thoughts effectively in English. Until these lessons have been learned, the writer cannot hope to succeed; and if they remain to be mastered along with the historical techniques, the path to achievement will be long and hard.

INTRODUCTION TO
RESEARCH IN AMERICAN HISTORY

INTRODUCTION TO
RESEARCH IN AMERICAN HISTORY

I. THE GATHERING OF DATA

1. CHOOSING A SUBJECT

In choosing a subject for investigation several considerations should be borne in mind. It is obvious that the writer must have an adequate acquaintance with the general field in which it falls; hence the importance of "background" courses and general reading. Or, to put the matter in the way in which it will usually present itself to a graduate student, the writer will be most likely to find a suitable topic within the scope of some one of the advanced subject-matter courses which he is pursuing. Moreover, if the topic lies in economic history, the writer must be acquainted with the principles of economics; if in diplomatic history, he should know the elements of international law and perhaps one or more foreign languages. Each topic requires its own type of preliminary training. Choice should be made of a subject in which interest has been aroused in the course of actual study—a theme which is clearly capable of further development through examination of tangible evidence, not an abstraction which can only be discussed speculatively.

The choice of topic should be made *by* the writer and not *for* him. The sense of responsibility for results will thus be awakened, and the topic will be more likely to interest the writer and to challenge his best efforts. The ideal to be aimed at throughout is a maximum of independent initiative and a minimum of direction. It is wise, however, to obtain the advice of a competent person in order to prevent an unfortunate selection. The adviser should prevent the choice of a theme for which the novice lacks proper preparation, or the scope of which is not properly defined, or for the treatment of which there is insufficient available material.

There is a natural tendency on the part of persons who are in the early stages of their experience to attempt studies the scope of which is too broad. It is not unusual for them to propose comprehensive surveys, such as "The Evolution of English Manners, Laws, and Customs from Anglo-Saxon Times to the Present." Studies in English law have occupied scholars for a lifetime, and such a project as the above, undertaken by a graduate student, say, with a few weeks, or at most months, at his command, would preclude any investigation beyond the taking of a few notes from the works of the masters. It must be remembered that the purpose of a first undertaking is to give the writer experience in the use of the historian's tools. It is consequently essential that the topic be of such a nature as to compel the investigator to go to the sources for a goodly portion of his data. The desideratum is a bit of intensive use of the techniques rather than a superficial survey and summary of the work of other writers, however excellent; and the scope of the project must be so restricted as to permit thorough treatment in the time available. It is therefore better, for example, to make a study of "Ohio in the Presidential Campaign of 1900" than to attempt to encompass "The History of Political Parties in the United States"; better to investigate "Sectionalism in the Tariff Debate of 1816" than to try to write a history either of "Sectionalism" or "The Tariff."

It is quite legitimate, nevertheless, to state the project in terms which may require limitation later when the theme is seen in clearer light. A proposal to study "The Attitude of Republican Leaders towards the Fourteenth Amendment" might serve well enough at the outset, but the abundance of material to be examined, or the time required to complete the original undertaking, or other conditions as revealed in the course of the labor on the project, might properly lead to a rewording, such as: "The Attitude of Republican Leaders towards the Fourteenth Amendment during the Debate on Its Passage," or "during the Congressional Campaign of 1866." Whatever the final form of statement may be, the topic must possess a unity of its own, and must be so delimited that all significant evidence bearing upon it may be carefully examined. These are the characteristics which must be shown by what is called a "monograph."

Even in the case of a first effort, there is no justification for wasting time upon a subject which has no intrinsic interest or importance. Moreover, the monograph should be an original study. It is wise, therefore, to choose a subject the exact ground of which has not been thoroughly covered by earlier writers, in order that one may be compelled to handle it along original lines. On the other hand, a writer who has initiative can often go over old ground and in the light of new evidence improve upon existing treatments.[1] Even a beginner should cultivate the attitude and habits of one who expects his study to be printed and read. In the case of doctoral dissertations publication is expected, and it happens not infrequently that master's theses are accepted in whole or in part by local history magazines.

2. THE STATUS OF THE MATERIALS FOR AMERICAN HISTORY

At the outset of an investigation it is important to ascertain what has already been written upon the subject. While a meritorious monograph must rest largely upon study of the sources, writings which are secondary from one point of view may be sources from another. Thus Roosevelt's *Winning of the West* is a secondary work on Western history, but if one were studying Roosevelt's methods and traits as a historian, it would, for that purpose, become a source. It is therefore necessary for the investigator to know both how to discover what has

---

[1] ". . . The student should cultivate the faculty of detecting facts overlooked by others, or new relationships in old facts. The mark of a gifted investigator is that he finds what he wants where others have never thought of looking, or have looked too superficially."—Allan Nevins, *Master's Essays in History*, 6.

been written on his theme, and how to find all of the additional material, especially the sources, bearing upon it. Both of these necessities call for the preparation of a list of books, articles, documents, manuscripts, and other materials.

The last century has been a period of great activity on the part of the leading nations in the collecting and publishing of their historical records. In the United States many agencies, both national and local, have engaged in enterprises of this sort. Governments—Federal, state, and municipal—have done much; many libraries, supported by Congress, state legislatures, cities, universities, historical societies, or private benefactions, have become the repositories of valuable collections. In spite of the fact that untold quantities of historical matter still lie hidden in the possession of unknown private owners, the accessible collections already immeasurably exceed the portions which have been carefully examined. Historians in this country are embarrassed by the very richness of their resources.

Another embarrassment of a very different but very serious nature arises from the scattered condition of the materials. Documents vital for the history of a state or region are as likely as not to be located in some remote repository. Thus manuscripts relating to many of the older states, from Virginia and the Carolinas westward and northwestward to the Mississippi and the Lakes, are in the possession of the Wisconsin Historical Society, at Madison. The Newberry Library at Chicago has many of the papers of Father Junipero Serra, the founder of the California missions. The papers of many public men are scattered among numerous libraries. This is true of those left by William Henry Harrison, for example. Illustrations might be multiplied.

The historian's gratitude is due to the pioneer collectors whose zeal preserved precious documents which might otherwise have been lost altogether. He is, none the less, often puzzled by the illogical location of materials which he may need, and fearful lest he fail to find some important body of them. There is no hope that the future will bring much improvement, by way of a sorting of state and national materials and a redistribution of them to the logical depositories; the rivalries of collecting institutions and the vested rights of possessors are too strong to permit such action. The utmost that can be hoped for is that copies of important documents (which can now be made quite cheaply by the use of the photostat) will be multiplied so that they may be possessed by every institution which has use for them, and that more and more adequate guides, catalogues, indexes, calendars, etc., will be prepared to give comprehensive information concerning the location, character, and value of materials of various kinds.

Much work has already been done along these lines, and much is being carried on at present. Most of the states have some agency—a historian, historical commission, department of history, historical library, or archives department—one of the principal duties of which is to acquire all possible matter relating to the history of the state, and to inform the public in appropriate publications of the scope of the collection and of other collections in or out of the state which have significance for its history.

The advanced investigator will need a fund of general information of this kind, as well as some knowledge of the great libraries of the country and a particular knowledge of the location of the chief collections in which he is directly interested. By way of illustration it may be mentioned that the Library of Congress is the largest collection of books in the United States and one of the largest in the world. Under the law, two copies of every copyrighted book must be deposited in the Library, which thus becomes automatically a complete collection of current American books. Books of foreign publication are also added constantly by purchase, gift, or exchange.

It is a particular function of the Library to acquire manuscripts relating to American history. It has had innumerable transcripts made of matter in foreign archives, and has accumulated a vast number of papers left by American statesmen. This part of its resources is also being constantly augmented.

Its collection of newspapers is more complete for many localities than the best collections in the localities themselves. On the side of publication it issues numerous calendars, checklists, and bibliographies.[2] For the historian, the resources of the Congressional Library exceed, on the whole, those of every other collection in the country, although for particular classes of material it does not always stand first.

Next to the Library of Congress in all-around utility for history is probably the library of Harvard University. For the history of the Confederacy and of the South in general, the Virginia State Library and the library of the University of Texas are most important. For the Rocky Mountain states and the Pacific Coast, the Bancroft Library of the University of California is unapproached, while for the early period in the upper Mississippi Valley and Old Northwest the Wisconsin Historical Society Library is unexcelled.

Most of the great libraries issue publications descriptive of their resources. Besides publications of this sort and those pertaining to particular states, there are a number of printed guides of general character. Among the more important are those prepared by the Library of Congress, the Carnegie Institution, and the American Historical Association.[3]

That materials are so badly scattered in illogical places, that so large a part of them is not published, and that the guides giving their location and character are none too adequate, are facts which concern every historian sooner or later. One who has reached the status of candidate for the degree of Doctor of Philosophy will spend some time in locating his materials, and when they have been found, may be compelled to go to them. The writer of a master's thesis will ordinarily work less with unpublished manuscripts than with printed documents, and as a rule will find everything that he needs in the library of any one of a score of universities. In any case, however, the investigator, in his quest for materials, will profit by a good technique.

[2] See pages 32, 39–41.
[3] See pages 38–39, 41–42.

3. THE TENTATIVE BIBLIOGRAPHY

No two subjects call for precisely the same procedure in the search for data, and the discussion of methodology must be more or less generalized because of these differences. Each writer must learn to select those aids which are appropriate for his special problem. Some of the first steps may nevertheless be clarified by a concrete illustration.

Let us suppose that a beginner has chosen "President Arthur and Civil Service Reform" as a subject for investigation. It is assumed that his background courses and general reading have familiarized him with the main features of political history, so that he understands the setting of his topic in the larger whole. If this is not the case, it will be necessary to examine the best secondary authorities who cover the seventies and eighties. It will be especially important to review the antecedent history of the particular topic, in this case involving a careful grounding in the origin and workings of the spoils system and the early stages of the reform movement.

a. *Items from the Library Catalogue*

As a first step towards the collection of material for the treatment of the theme, the student must prepare a working bibliography to be used as a guide to the books, articles, documents, and other writings to be examined. In making such a bibliography, it is the impulse of most persons to begin with the card catalogue of the library in which the work is to be done. This is perhaps as good a way as any to make a beginning.

i. THE DICTIONARY CATALOGUE DESCRIBED

Effective use of a library demands a knowledge of the system of classification and cataloguing employed. There are several types of catalogue, and the investigator must acquaint himself with the one used in the institution in which he works. Nowadays the dictionary catalogue is so much more common than any other kind that it is the only type that will be described.[4]

[4] For a fuller description of library catalogues, see Margaret Hutchins, *et al.*, *Guide to the Use of Libraries.*

In this type of catalogue all main entries are arranged in one alphabet, much as words are in a dictionary. Every book is represented by several cards: one is filed under the surname of the author of the book, another under the first word (not an article) of the title, and a varying number under appropriate subject headings. One subject card may indicate the nature of the whole book, another a topic given prominence in a part of it, and others bibliographies, biographies, or critiques which it contains. Still other cards may be filed under the names of editors, translators, compilers, joint authors, and the series title, if there is one. Under subject entries cross reference cards are used, in addition, to call attention to other subject entries under which related works may be found (as, under CIVIL SERVICE one might find a cross reference reading See SPOILS SYSTEM). Cross references are also used to refer from an author's pen name to his real name.

While all main entries appear in one alphabet, some of the entries have subdivisions within which the items are arranged in a subordinate alphabet, because such groups of cards have a unity of their own. Thus under the letter U will be found a main heading UNITED STATES as *author*. Here are listed in alphabetical order (1) all publications issued by the Department of Agriculture; (2) those published by the department or bureau next in alphabetical order, *e.g.*, the Bureau of Animal Industry (the determining word here being *Animal*); (3) those of the Bureau of Biological Survey, etc.

Then follows another main entry—UNITED STATES as *subject*— with similar subdivisions, such as ARMY, CENSUS, COMMERCE, EDUCATION, HISTORY, etc. Under HISTORY again there are many subdivisions, according to period, topic, or geographical section. This process of subalphabetization is capable of indefinite extension. Many of the cards in these subdivisions duplicate, of course, those in the primary alphabet.

There are certain other departures from a strictly one-alphabet arrangement in the dictionary catalogue. For example, all names beginning with New as a *word* precede all which begin

with New as a *syllable*. Thus New Albany is followed by New
Jersey and New York before Newark appears; New Zealand
precedes Newald. A series of identical names of persons, as
John Smith, are filed in the order of the birth-dates of the
persons. If the same word is the name of a person, place, and
thing, the respective cards are filed in this order, the name of the
person before that of the place, etc.[5]

Guide cards which project slightly above the entry cards and
bear subjects and names are inserted at frequent intervals in the
catalogue, to facilitate the finding of desired entries.

ii. USE OF SUBJECT ENTRIES

It is evident that even if one is not acquainted with the names
of many authors or the titles of many books related to one's
topic (as may well be the case at the beginning of an investigation), one may compile quite a bibliography by a skillful use of
subject entries. In the assumed case of a student investigating
"President Arthur and Civil Service Reform," it would be
naïve to look for a catalogue entry with that exact wording.
But subject entries would undoubtedly be found under both
CHESTER A. ARTHUR and CIVIL SERVICE. Knowing as a background fact that the act passed during Arthur's administration
is called the Pendleton Act, it should occur to the student to
look under GEORGE H. PENDLETON for additional clues. Knowing also that George William Curtis, Dorman B. Eaton, and
others whose names should readily come to mind, were prominent in the reform movement, and that Presidents Grant and
Hayes were concerned with the early attempts to administer
reform legislation, he would list the biographies of these men and
any other promising titles found under their names. The more
thorough the grounding in general history, and the more numer-

---

[5] Many libraries use in their catalogues cards printed by the Library of
Congress primarily for its own catalogue and secondarily for distribution. Only
one form of card—the author card—is printed for each book. The purchasing
library obtains the requisite number of duplicates and adds all needed headings
in the blank space above the author's name.

ous the cognate subjects in the investigator's mind, the greater
the number of clues that will be found in this way.

Bibliographies are often to be found listed under subject headings, and are of especial value in compiling the tentative bibliography.[6]

iii. FORMS FOR NOTES ON BIBLIOGRAPHY

Care should be taken to systematize procedure from the very
start. When the examination of the card catalogue is begun, the
investigator should be supplied with slips of paper on each of
which one item (and one only) may be entered. The size of these
slips is a matter of individual preference or convenience; the
plan first tried is often changed in the light of experience. Many
persons use 3 x 5-inch cards, which is the size found in the
library catalogue. Others prefer larger cards or slips. Stationers
can supply cards of several standard sizes, as well as cabinets
in which they may be filed, varying from inexpensive pasteboard
trays to large metal cases. Many workers do not use cards at
all, but make their notes on bibliography and subject-matter
on slips or sheets of paper of uniform size. Slips half the size
of a sheet of typewriter letter paper are quite satisfactory in the
long run, and the uniform size permits all notes to be filed in one
cabinet. Small cards do not afford much space for subject-
matter notes, and large ones are too costly, since notes frequently require only a few words. The use of two cabinets of
different sizes, one for bibliography cards and one for subject-
matter notes, is likely to prove inconvenient.

When the library catalogue yields the first useful bibliographical item, it should be entered on a slip. Suppose that the
student looked first under CIVIL SERVICE and found there a
card for the book by Carl Russell Fish entitled *The Civil Service
and the Patronage*. In making his own slip he should include, so
far as possible, every scrap of information bearing on the value
of this book for his investigation and all of the data which he
will need if the book finds a place in his final bibliography.

[6] See page 24.

The general authoritativeness of a work is often indicated in a superficial way by the author's position, and any available data of this kind should be noted either at the bottom of the slip or on the back. Thus it would be well to note that the author of the book just mentioned is a professor of history in the University of Wisconsin (a fact which could be ascertained by consulting *Who's Who in America*).[7] This fact in itself gives assurance that the book is the work of a trained historian. A cursory examination of the volume will reveal that it covers the whole period from Washington's presidency to the close of the nineteenth century. A note to this effect should be placed on the slip. Finally, if any portion of the volume bears directly upon the student's theme, the chapter and pages should be set down.

Notes of this kind are in the nature of comment, and should be distinguished from bibliographical data proper. Each book placed in the final bibliography should be described or identified by the inclusion of the following data, so far as applicable to it: (1) Name of author, editor, or compiler, in full, with the family name preceding the given name; (2) exact title as it appears on the title page (not cover) of the book, down to the word *by* which precedes the name of the author; (3) the identification of the edition if there is more than one; (4) the number of volumes if there is more than one; (5) the name of the publisher; (6) the place of publication (the home office when more than one place is named on the title page); (7) the date of publication.

If there is more than one volume and they have been issued at different times, the dates of the appearance of the first and last should be indicated thus: 1882–1888. If the publication is still in progress, that fact is indicated by leaving the second date blank, thus: 1928–   . If the date of publication does not appear on the title page, the copyright date from the following

---

[7] Published biennially by A. N. Marquis & Co., Chicago. *Who's Who* lists only living persons, although by running back through the series of volumes biographical facts are ascertainable about many persons now deceased. *The Dictionary of American Biography*, edited by Allen Johnson and Dumas Malone, and now in process of publication, will be the best source of information about nonliving Americans when it is completed.

page may be substituted, thus: [c1928]. If that too is wanting, the abbreviation n. d. (no date) should be used. If the date or dates of publication are supplied from external sources they should be inclosed in brackets, without the c, thus: [1928–1930]. If no place of publication is given, that fact is indicated by using n. p. (no place). If the place of publication is supplied by the writer, it should be inclosed in brackets to indicate that it is interpolated, thus: [Albany].

It was formerly a frequent practice to omit the publisher's name from a bibliographical entry, but it is advisable to include it as one of the best means of identifying the publication. Some authors give it before the place and some after; the practice of publishers also varies, as may be seen by examining a few title pages. The natural place seems to be before the name of the city or town, just as in the case of ordinary addresses of persons.

Catalogue cards contain other information of various kinds, such as the number of pages in the book, the size of the page, and whether there are maps or illustrations. Ordinarily these are of no significance for the historian and need not be recorded in his notes. It will save time, however, in obtaining volumes again, if the call number is placed on the slip.

The slip for Fish's book, when made out in accordance with these suggestions, would appear as follows:

Special Monographs

AH5   Fish, Carl Russell,
H33   The Civil Service and the Patronage (Harvard Histor-
v.11   ical Studies, XI).
      Longmans, Green and Company, New York, 1905.
      [Author is prof. of hist. in U. of Wis. Book covers 1789–
      1901. Ch. X on "Civil Service Reform, 1865–1901."
      Pp. 217–222 on Arthur's presidency. Bibliog., 252–266.]

In the foregoing form, the underscoring of certain words in written or typewritten work indicates that they should be italicized when printed. If proper underscoring and other matters of form are carefully practiced from the beginning, the later task of mastering the rules governing footnotes and final bibliography will be simplified.

If a volume is one of a series by different authors under a common editor or series title, the note should be made for the *volume* used and its relation to the series should be indicated as follows:

General Histories
Sparks, Edwin Erle,
National Development, 1877–1885 (volume XXIII of The American Nation, edited by Albert Bushnell Hart).
Harper and Brothers, New York, 1907.

Each work found by using the catalogue should be promptly examined in order to ascertain whether the promise of usefulness given by the title is likely to be fulfilled. After a few titles have been listed, it is advisable to go to the shelves in the book stacks and actually handle the books one by one. This may require a stack permit, for which application must be made to the library officials. If the volumes are not to be found where they are sought, the attendants will give aid in tracing them. Examination will show that some of them bear intimately upon the investigation, while others have no important relation to it and may be discarded from the tentative bibliography. The probable importance of each should be indicated in the comments entered on the slip. (In the case of the form for Fish's book, such an examination is assumed to have been made, as the basis of the sample comments.) While looking over the books on the shelves it is well also to glance at the adjacent shelves, as it is possible that other useful books may be found there, which have escaped attention during the use of the catalogue.

The appraisal of books at this stage is necessarily superficial. The novice should be diffident as to the soundness of his own judgment concerning their worth, and should seek expert opinion. There are several ways to obtain it. For books published before the close of the nineteenth century, Larned's *Literature of American History* may be consulted.[8] This volume lists 4145

[8] Wherever, as here, full bibliographical data for books mentioned in the text are not given in the footnotes, they will be found in the bibliography at the end of this manual.

of the books on American history most likely to be found in libraries, and for each gives a brief statement of merits or demerits, written by a competent critic. Supplements for the years 1900, 1901, 1902, 1903, and 1904 give similar estimates of a few current publications.

In general the most reliable comment on books is to be found in the critiques, commonly called reviews, published by the leading magazines—and especially, of course, for historical works, those which appear in the leading historical periodicals, such as the *American Historical Review*. It is a rather tedious task to run down critiques of particular books, although the fact that they usually appear from six to eighteen months after the publication of the volumes reviewed is of some help in narrowing the range of the search. To some extent reviews have been indexed in the indexes to periodical literature.[9] For the years since publication began, the *Book Review Digest* is especially useful. It is a monthly publication, dating from 1905, which condenses book reviews from more than fifty English and American periodicals. A sentence or two, or a plus or minus sign (for favorable and unfavorable judgments) indicates the trend of opinion, while specific references guide the student to the issues of the periodicals where the reviews are published.

iv. FILING OF NOTES ON BIBLIOGRAPHY

As the collection of slips grows, it will be necessary to adopt a plan of classification and to arrange them in accordance with it. The worker who yields to the temptation to copy a number of titles on one sheet of paper needlessly deprives himself of a valuable device for saving labor, since each title must be copied on a separate slip before it can be filed in its proper place. The scheme of classification should be elastic and subject to modification as the concept of the topic enlarges. Before filing the slips a heading should be written at the top of each, above the author's name, indicating the character of the work with relation to the task in hand. If these headings should later prove illogical,

[9] See page 28 *et seq.*

or unsatisfactory for any reason, the separate slips make re-arrangement easy.

One tentative division of the bibliography may be headed "General Histories." Here might be filed the book by Sparks, cited in the foregoing illustration. Another division might be called "Special Monographs." Fish's study would belong here (see form above).

If cards are used for the bibliography, it is advisable to use guides, similar to the guide cards in the catalogue, for these divisions and subdivisions. Guides of one color may be used for the main divisions, and of other colors for subdivisions.

b. *Items from Bibliographies and Footnotes in Books*

The examination of the library catalogue having been completed, the next step in the building of the tentative bibliography is to examine the bibliographies and footnotes in the books found by this means. In this way the authors and titles of many more books may be learned, and clues may be obtained to other kinds of materials. This part of the work may be done with economy of time while the books are being examined and appraised as already described. However, if the search for additional bibliographical data tends to confuse and complicate the process of appraisal, it will be wise to leave this further quest to be undertaken as a separate process.

i. CONCERNING OTHER BOOKS

Citations obtained by the examination of books should be entered on slips in the way that has been described. It may prove helpful to add a note showing where the citation was found. If one obtained from the bibliography on pages 252–266 of Fish, *The Civil Service and the Patronage*, the following item, the location in Fish's book might be noted thus:

> Bernard, George,
> Civil Service Reform versus the Spoils System.
> J. B. Alden, New York, 1885.
> [Fish, C. S. & P., bib.]

The forms used by some writers differ somewhat from those recommended in this manual, which follows the practice of the American Historical Association in its publications; but carefully prepared bibliographies, such as the one in Fish's volume, usually give all of the data needed, with the exception sometimes of the publisher's name. Footnotes, however, do not usually give the data, for their purpose is not primarily bibliographical.[10] One encounters, for instance, in a footnote on page 216 of Fish, a reference to Lambert, *Progress of Civil Service Reform in the United States*, and it is necessary to turn to the bibliography for fuller information about the work. There, under the division headed PAMPHLETS AND OTHER CONTEMPORARY DISCUSSION, are found the data for the following bibliographical note (here the publisher's name is lacking, and if supplied must be learned from some other source):

> Lambert, Henry,
> Progress of Civil Service Reform in the United States. Boston, 1885.
> [Fish, C. S. & P., bib.]

Items added to the tentative bibliography by this method must in due time be examined and appraised in the same way as those found by using the catalogue. If reference is found to a book which the library does not possess, a note to that effect should be included in the comment. If it is a book which appears to be of considerable value in the investigation, the library will perhaps purchase it upon request, or upon the recommendation of the Department of History. If it is out of print and not obtainable by purchase, it may be possible to borrow it for a brief time through the system of inter-library loans. The library officials or the History Department should be consulted in such cases. Books not actually used in writing the monograph should ordinarily not be listed in the final bibliography, unless they appear to be of especial importance, in which case they may be

---

[10] For discussion of the difference between footnotes and bibliography, see pages 126–129.

included with a comment explaining both the apparent value and the reasons for the failure to make use of them.

ii. CONCERNING PERIODICAL ARTICLES AND NEWSPAPER DATA

Besides book titles, the examination of bibliographies and footnotes should bring to light titles of articles in periodicals, newspaper items, matter in government documents, and miscellaneous sources of information. To materials of these kinds the directions for listing books are not altogether applicable. Suppose that one finds somewhere a footnote reference to an article printed in a periodical. As in the case of a book, the footnote citation may be in abbreviated form, necessitating examination of the bibliography or the magazine itself to obtain the data for such an entry as the following: [11]

> Cary, Edward,
> "The Administration and Civil Service Reform." International
> Review, VI, 227–233 (March, 1879).

It is to be noted that the underscoring for italics in citations of periodical literature is confined to the name of the *periodical*, while the title of the article is inclosed in quotation marks. The data concerning publisher and place of publication, required in the case of books, are replaced by the citation of the volume of the magazine, the page limits of the article, and the date of the issue of the number in which the article appears. Appropriate headings, comments on the author and the character and value of the article, as well as a note showing where the item was found, should be added in these entries, just as in the case of books.

This same form may be employed in citing encyclopedia articles, but between the name of the encyclopedia and the volume containing the article the number of the edition should be given for purposes of identification, thus: *Encyclopædia Britannica*, 14th ed., XI, etc.

[11] It will be increasingly necessary to depart from the hypothetical student investigating the Civil Service, in order to find suitable illustrations of the manifold aspects of the search for data. No one topic involves all of the points which require illustration or discussion.

Articles in the reports, annuals, and studies published by universities, historical societies, and other learned organizations are usually listed like those in periodicals when they do not fill entire volumes:

> Bassett, John Spencer,
> "The Regulators of North Carolina (1765–1771)." American Historical Association Report for 1894, 141–212.

> Esarey, Logan,
> "The Organization of the Jacksonian Party in Indiana." Mississippi Valley Historical Association Proceedings for 1913–1914, pp. 220–243.

In these items the names of the organizations are not italicized, but only the words which are regarded as the titles of the publications which appear periodically, *i.e.*, *Report* and *Proceedings*. In calling at a delivery desk for either of the articles used in the illustrations, one could probably not use the name of the author or the title of the article, but would have to ask for the *Report* or *Proceedings* of the organization concerned, for the year in question, just as in calling for a magazine in which a desired article was printed it would be necessary to give the date of the issue or the number of the volume.

However, if the entire volume is devoted to one study, the title of the study should be underscored like a book title, instead of being placed in quotation marks, as is done in the case of articles:

> Gephart, William F.,
> Transportation and Industrial Development in the Middle West (Columbia University Studies in Economics, History, and Public Law, XXXIV).
> Columbia University, New York, 1912.

> Houston, David Franklin,
> A Critical Study of Nullification in South Carolina (Harvard Historical Studies, III).
> Longmans, Green & Co., New York, 1898.

In these illustrations the titles of the series in which the monographs appear are italicized, as well as the monograph titles. In the first illustration, however, the series title does not include the name of the university, while in the second it does. Such variations are, of course, very confusing to the student, and make absolute accuracy and consistency of form almost impossible.

The parts of a composite volume are often catalogued separately. This is quite likely to be true in the case of university studies, several of which are often bound together. In such cases each study is given its distinctive number when it is cited. In general the form used in listing essays in such composite books is similar to that followed for periodical articles:

Adams, Herbert Baxter,
"Maryland's Influence upon Land Cessions" (Johns Hopkins University Studies in History and Political Science, III, No. 1).
Johns Hopkins University, Baltimore, 1885.

Becker, Carl Lotus,
"Kansas," in Essays in American History Dedicated to Frederick Jackson Turner, 85-111.
Henry Holt and Company, New York, 1910.

Chandler, William E.,
"Chester A. Arthur," in The Presidents of the United States, 1789-1914, by John Fiske . . . and many others, ed. by James Grant Wilson, III, 195-237.
Charles Scribner's Sons, New York, 1914.

In taking references to newspapers, the name of the paper as it is printed on the first page should be given, in italics, and also the date of the issue in which the item is printed. If the name of the paper does not indicate the home of the publication, it (state or city as needed) should be interpolated in parentheses. This is not necessary, however, in the case of the weekly and monthly news magazines of wide circulation, such as the *Review of Reviews*, *Nation*, and *Literary Digest*. The nature of each item should be noted, an editorial being distinguished from a news item or a communication from a private correspondent, etc. In this class of citations it is particularly important to note the work from which the reference is taken, if not obtained directly from the newspaper, since credit must be given to that work if the item is used.[12] Examples:

The New York Times, Dec. 18, 1895.
   [Editorial on Pres. Cleveland's message on Venezuelan boundary dispute.]

Baltimore Sun, July 6–11, 1904.
   [Report of the Dem. Nat. Nom. Convn. Cited by J. H. Latané, Am. as a World Power, 232.]

Public Opinion, XIX, 541, 552, 547, 586, 649.
   [Extracts from press comment on the Venezuelan boundary dispute, summer and fall, 1895. Cited, D. R. Dewey, Natl. Problems, 307.]

Springfield Republican (Mass.), Feb. 3, 1890.
   [Ed. comment on conduct of Reed as Speaker. Cited, Dewey, Natl. Probs., 154.]

The Christian Science Monitor (Boston), July 8, 1929.
   [Comments.]

iii. CONCERNING GOVERNMENT PUBLICATIONS

Footnotes which are found on those pages of books where the investigator's special subject is discussed, as on pages 217 to 222 of Fish's book if he is studying the civil service under Arthur, are of great value in the early stages of his work, while he is getting his bearings. Such notes often cite the exact location in the sources where the bills, acts, reports, or speeches are printed which form the heart of the subject. It is wise to take these citations as given, disregarding for the time the form in which they will be entered in the final bibliography, unless the data for it are right at hand.

No publications of the Federal Government are more often cited than those which contain the reports of debates in Congress.[13] Numerous references of which the student will need to make note will be found in forms like these:

---

[12] The proper forms for citations in footnotes will be considered later. See pages 122–123.
[13] See page 33.

Congressional Record, 47 Cong., 2 sess., 283, 463–464.
Congressional Record, 47 Cong., 1 sess., 5704, 6016; 2 sess., 204–
208, 241, 284, 316, 318; Congressional Globe, 41 Cong., 3 sess.,
1936.

A glance at the context on the pages where these citations
occur will indicate the topic to which they relate, and will
suggest appropriate headings and comments for the slips, which
may be taken in the following form:[14]

Pendleton Act
Senate Debate, 1882. Cong. Rec., 47 Cong., 2 sess., 283, 463–464.
[Fish, C. S. &. P., 218.]

Pendleton Act
Senate Debate, 1882. Cong. Rec., 47 Cong., 1 sess., 5704, 6016;
2 sess., 204–208, 241, 284, 316, 318. *Cf.* Cong. Globe, 41 Cong.,
3 sess., 1936.
[Fish, 219.]

Hints of pertinent matter in documents of various kinds,
which might otherwise be overlooked, may be caught from
footnotes:

Discussion of Pendleton Act
55 Cong., 2 sess., Sen. Doc. I, No. 24
[Fish, 220.]

Text of Pendleton Act
Stat. at Large, XXII, 403–407.
[Fish, 221.]

Arthur's Reform Message of Dec. 6, 1881.
Richardson, Messages, VIII, 11, 60.

Examination of other books will yield similar items, in random
order, making the usefulness of separate slips apparent, since
the related slips can be brought together in filing:

Campaign Assessments
Cong. Rec., 47 Cong., 2 sess., 141–143.
[Speech of Sen. Hale in defence of practice of levying camp.
assess. on office holders.] Sparks, Natl. Devel., 197.

Garfield's Message concerning Appointments and Removals.
Richardson, Messages and Papers, VIII, 147. [Sparks, 188.]

[14] Note that in citations of debates in Congress, Arabic numerals denote
columns instead of *pages.*

The two citations of presidential messages, both in a work associated with the name Richardson, suggest that certain classes of source material of government origin have been collected, edited, and published under government auspices. Among these classes are the messages of the presidents, the laws, the decisions of the courts, treaties with foreign nations, and other documents relating to foreign affairs. After encountering a few references to such publications the investigator will perceive the necessity of obtaining the full bibliographical data for them. In many cases this can be done readily by referring to the bibliographies in the works in which the footnote citations are found; and in addition to the specific citations which have been noted, a slip should be prepared for the entire collection, for example:

Richardson, James Daniel, comp.,
A Compilation of the Messages and Papers of the Presidents, 1789–1897. 10 vols.
Government Printing Office, Washington, 1896–1900.

Similarly, numerous references to the *Statutes at Large of the United States* will probably be gathered, such as:

Act Forbidding Campaign Contributions by Federal Employés
Stat. at Large, XIX, 169 (1876).
[Sparks, 197.]

A slip for this collection will sooner or later be prepared in this form:

The Statutes at Large of the United States . . . 1789–1873. 17 vols.
Little and Brown (later Little, Brown and Company), Boston, 1845–1873.

The Statutes at Large of the United States . . . 1873–   .
Volume 18, et seq.
Government Printing Office, Washington, 1875–   .

As citations of court decisions are picked up they may be noted thus:

De Lima v. Bidwell, 182 U. S., 1.
[Status of Porto Rico after cession to U. S. Applicability of tariff to imports from the island. Latané, Am. as a World Power, 145.]

It may here be explained that the manner of citing the decisions of the Federal Supreme Court long ago became conventionalized in the form given. In contrast with the usual practice of placing the volume designation *after* the title (as, *History of the United States*, VI, 142), Arabic figures denoting the volume *precede* the title in citations of the reports, and the page figures follow the title. Thus 182 U. S., 1, is equivalent to *Reports of the Supreme Court of the United States*, CLXXXII, 1. The conventional form has the obvious advantage of brevity. Previous to 1875, the name of the reporter was commonly used in place of the initials U. S.; thus 8 Cranch, 49, is equivalent to Cranch, reporter, *Decisions of the Supreme Court*, VIII, 49.[15]

iv. IMPORTANT BIBLIOGRAPHIES IN COMPREHENSIVE HISTORIES

The foregoing are examples of the kinds of references which may be gleaned from footnotes and bibliographies in monographs. While for the student of a particular theme the bibliographies in works on related subjects are of special importance, it should be borne in mind that some of the general histories contain bibliographical data of immense value. The chief materials relating to almost every phase of American history prior to 1789 are discussed in the "Critical Essays on the Sources of Information" which follow each chapter of Justin Winsor's *Narrative and Critical History of America* (last volume published in 1889).

Suppose the topic under investigation to be The Stamp Act Controversy. On pages 72 and following, in the sixth volume of Winsor's work (as is readily ascertained by use of the index) are given exhaustive references to sources of all kinds on that subject, so far as they had been brought together by the historical scholarship of Winsor's day. Of course, since the publication

[15] The observant reader will have noticed some irregularities in the sample forms. Thus in one place the phrase Government Printing Office may appear in full, while in another it may be abbreviated. The forms are to illustrate the use of slips by the investigator, and so long as they contain the needed data in form intelligible to him they serve their purpose. Precision and uniformity are highly desirable, however, when the citations are made in the finished monograph. Even there constantly repeated names and titles may be abbreviated.

of this work there have been discoveries of sources, and critical studies, which must be sought by other means.

Useful in the same way as Winsor's essays, but less detailed, are the "Critical Essays on Authorities" which form the last chapters in each volume of Albert Bushnell Hart's series entitled *The American Nation: A History*, and the similar essays which form concluding chapters in the volumes of the new series, *A History of American Life*, edited by Arthur M. Schlesinger and Dixon Ryan Fox.

The more obvious and accessible references for many topics are given in Channing, Hart, and Turner's *Guide to the Reading and Study of American History*, a work which has many other valuable features besides.

c. *Use of Existing Bibliographies*

While examining subject entries in the dictionary catalogue, the investigator is likely to find references to bibliographies of his topic or related subjects. Thus under CIVIL SERVICE he will probably discover the following:

> Civil Service Reform Association,
> Bibliography of Civil Service Reform and Related Subjects.
> Published for the Women's Auxiliary to the Civil Service Reform Association, New York, 1900.

Any such work would, of course, be carefully examined for references not otherwise obtained. The investigator may be well repaid for his pains, or, as in the present instance (assuming the student seeking references on Arthur's term), may find but few useful references. The cards in the catalogue under UNITED STATES as *author*, Library of Congress, Division of Bibliography, should also be inspected, and may or may not reveal the existence of a "Select List of References" on the subject—to use the favorite term employed by the division in titles of bibliographies. Other divisions of the Library of Congress issue useful lists which should be looked for, notably the Division of Maps and Manuscripts.

One of the best methods of discovering bibliographies of

subjects under investigation, if any exist, is to consult the section on Bibliography in the annual volumes entitled *Writings on American History*. However, this work, which is described more fully later,[16] lists no publications issued prior to 1902. For older bibliographies it is well to consult the indexes to periodicals described below, especially the *Annual Literary Index* and its successors.[17] Edith M. Coulter, in her *Guide to Historical Bibliographies*, lists bibliographies by countries, periods, and states, checklists and catalogues of special collections of material, and some bibliographies of specific topics.

By the use of these and similar aids the student of the Stamp Act Controversy, for example, should eventually discover that a bibliography on the Act and kindred legislation is printed in a *Bulletin of the New York Public Library*, and from this Bulletin he would learn further of little known pamphlets on the subject in the library of the New York Historical Society.

d. *Other Aids in Finding Materials*

Some of the works now to be discussed relate no more closely to the work of the historian than to that of investigators in other fields; others deal with matters which primarily concern students of social science. In the first group belongs the book compiled by Isadore G. Mudge, and entitled *New Guide to Reference Books*. It may be referred to for further information about many of the guides, indexes, and aids discussed in the following paragraphs.

i. GENERAL CATALOGUES OF BOOKS

Several attempts have been made to compile comprehensive dictionaries or catalogues of books published in the United States. Complete files of these catalogues are not likely to be found except in a few of the larger libraries of the country, so that their accessibility for use by graduate students is somewhat restricted.

---

[16] See page 41 *et seq.*   [17] See page 29.

For books published before 1820 the most important of these comprehensive catalogues is that prepared by Charles Evans, under the title *American Bibliography*. Its purpose is to list in chronological order of publication all books, pamphlets, and periodicals printed in the English continental colonies and the United States from 1639 to 1820, and to give full bibliographical data for each. Ten volumes have been issued (1930), bringing the compilation down to the year 1796. Each volume contains a classified subject index. Most of the publications listed are now out of print and quite rare, making very useful the information given as to libraries in which copies are to be found.

An earlier undertaking of similar kind but even greater scope is that begun by Joseph Sabin under the title *Dictionary of Books Relating to America from its Discovery to the Present Time*. This work is also known by the half-title: *Bibliotheca Americana*. It was designed to include books, pamphlets, and periodicals printed in America, and those about America published in foreign lands. The arrangement is in the alphabetical order of author's names. The first volume appeared in 1868, and the nineteenth in 1892, bringing the *Dictionary* to the name Simms. At that point the work was interrupted for many years, but it was resumed in the early 1920's by Mr. Wilberforce Eames. Volume XXI, bringing the entries to the name William Smith, was issued in 1929. Like the Evans *Bibliography*, this *Dictionary* frequently names libraries which possess copies of rare books.

The title *Bibliotheca Americana* had been used before Sabin by Orville Augustus Roorbach, who during the years 1852–1861 published four volumes cataloguing American books published after 1820. It is thus clear why Evans, whose project was taken up later, set 1820 as his terminal date. Roorbach's enterprise was continued by James Kelly, in two volumes entitled *American Catalogue of Books Published in the United States from January, 1861, to January, 1871*. The final product in this series was the *American Catalogue of Books*, which appeared in successive issues from 1876 to 1910. The first issue listed books in print (that is, offered for sale by the publishers) on July 1, 1876, and the later volumes recorded books published during successive intervals thereafter.

The *American Catalogue* was compiled by cumulating in one alphabet the entries in the *Publishers' Weekly*, a trade journal which first appeared in 1872. The *Weekly* provides an excellent means of keeping in touch with current books, as each number contains a list of the week's issues, as well as announcements of forthcoming books. From 1886 to 1910 there was an intermediate form, of temporary value, known as the *Annual American Catalogue*.

The *Publishers' Weekly* is still the standard journal of the American book trade, but the *American Catalogue* has given place to the *United States Catalogue*, published by the H. W. Wilson Company of New York, which during the last generation has become the chief producer of library guides and indexes. The *United States Catalogue* made its bow in 1900, with an issue listing books in print in that year. Later issues catalogue new publications during periods of three or five years, thus forming a continuous and complete record. The subject entries are of great value in compiling bibliographies, and the data given are complete and very accurate. At intervals volumes have been devoted, like the first, to cataloguing books in print at specified dates. The latest of these lists books in print on January 1, 1928. It includes not only the output of commercial concerns, but works printed privately, regular importations, Canadian books which are not also published south of the Border, university, society, and state publications, and those of the Smithsonian Institution, the National Museum, the Bureau of American Ethnology, and some other government departments and agencies, both Federal and state.

The *Cumulative Book Index*, a monthly periodical issued by the same publishers, bears much the same relation to the *United States Catalogue* that the *Publishers' Weekly* formerly did to the *American Catalogue*. Certain issues are cumulative, the most important being the annual numbers which bridge the years between the volumes of the *United States Catalogue*.

A recent work limited to books on history is *A Guide to Historical Literature*. It is a product of coöperation, and was brought out under the auspices of the American Historical Association by a committee headed by Professor George M. Dutcher. It lists and appraises the chief historical writings of all types, all times, and all countries, and includes carefully selected bibliographies.

ii. INDEXES OF PERIODICAL LITERATURE

Much of the best work of investigators finds its first expression in print in the form of articles in periodicals, both of the general and professional classes; and it is quite necessary to know how to ascertain expeditiously whether anything of significance for one's study has appeared in them. Considering the number and variety of these publications and the random order in which, necessarily, their offerings are made to the public, it would seem that every separate article of their contents was doomed to early oblivion in the vast total of their output. Even the indexes which each periodical provides at regular intervals help but little, for it is utterly impracticable to run through the annual indexes of *The Century Magazine*, *Harper's Magazine*, *The Atlantic Monthly*, and a score of others, in the faint hope of finding some contribution related to one's investigation. This situation, which yearly becomes more aggravated, would soon become utterly hopeless were it not for the comprehensive indexes.

The pioneer attempt to index American periodicals was begun in the 1880's, by William Frederick Poole. The first volume of what is known as *Poole's Index to Periodical Literature* was brought out in 1882, but reappeared in revised form in 1892. The two volumes of the work supplied a subject index of the contents of the most important American and English periodicals from 1802 to 1881.[18] Five supplements under the original

[18] It is of interest to note, in connection with the hypothetical study of President Arthur and Civil Service Reform, that the first volume of *Poole's Index* (1882) lists about one hundred articles discussing some phase of the civil service problem. *Cf.* Fish, *op. cit.*, 217.

title were prepared by Poole and others, with the coöperation of the American Library Association, each covering four or five years, and bringing the *Index* down to the close of 1906. In its entirety the *Index* covers a period of 105 years, and lists a total of nearly 600,000 articles in more than 12,000 volumes of nearly 500 periodicals. An abridged edition, sometimes called the "Baby Poole," was printed in 1901, covering all articles in a selected list of 37 periodicals which were still running at the close of 1899. One supplement to the abridgment appeared in 1905, covering the years 1900–1904.

The basis of the later supplements to *Poole's Index* was the *Annual Literary Index*, which ran from 1892 to 1904. Each volume included an author index, which is still of some utility, because Poole lacked this feature. Of chief present-day value, however, are the lists of bibliographies, and the indexes of dates of principal events. The latter may be used as a guide to the exact issues of newspapers in which accounts of important events may be found.

In 1905 the character of this publication was changed somewhat and its name altered to *Annual Library Index*. In this form it ran through six volumes, featuring an author, title, and subject index to periodicals, lists of bibliographies, and the index to dates. It was in turn superseded in 1912 by the *American Library Annual*, which ran through another five years (to 1917) with the same features minus the periodical index, which by this time was being cared for through the expansion of the *Readers' Guide* (*q. v.*).

Meantime, in 1896, the publication of the *Cumulative Index* had been undertaken by the Cleveland Public Library. It was issued monthly, and indexed some fifty periodicals by authors, titles, and subjects of articles. It was consolidated with the *Readers' Guide* in July, 1903, but it is still useful because it covered some magazines which Poole did not index.

The *Readers' Guide to Periodical Literature*, although a comparatively late comer, was destined eventually to become the leading publication of this class. Its first issue, in 1901, indexed only fifteen popular periodicals, but the scope of its operations was rapidly extended. In 1903, as has been said, it absorbed the *Cumulative Index*, and in 1911 it took over the index feature of the *Annual Library Index*. At about that time the discontinuance of the publication of the supplements to Poole left the field almost wholly to the *Readers' Guide*, with consequent further extension of its activities.

The primary form of the *Readers' Guide* is a monthly publication. The March, June, September, and December issues of each year cumulate all previous entries of the year in one dictionary catalogue. The last is thus an annual which serves as a semi-permanent index for the year, until superseded by the permanent cumulations issued at intervals of from three to five years. The first of these covered the years 1900–1904, and the latest, the seventh, the years 1925–1929.

In 1916 the first of the *Supplements* was issued, to provide for the additional work imposed by the discontinuance of Poole and features of the *Annual Library Index*. This new work necessitated the indexing of certain periodicals from 1907 on. The total number of articles already indexed in the permanent volumes of the *Readers' Guide* and *Supplements* considerably exceeds a million, and the periodicals covered include not only the most important general publications but many of the more prominent professional journals, such as the *American Historical Review* and the *American Political Science Review*.

Beginning in 1921, the name of the *Supplement* was changed to the *International Index to Periodicals*, because it covers some seventy-five foreign periodicals as well as more than one hundred domestic publications. Five issues appear yearly, the January number cumulating the entries for the preceding year. Permanent cumulations are issued at longer intervals.

Supplementing all of the above is the *Magazine Subject-Index*, a volume published in 1908. It was a subject index of seventy-nine American and English journals which neither Poole, the *Annual Library Index*, nor the *Readers' Guide* had covered. Of the seventy-nine, more than half were indexed from their first issues. The peculiar importance of this index for the historian lies in the fact that about one-half of the entries relate to history, especially to local history. In the annual continuations (*Annual Magazine Subject-Index*) this emphasis on history is maintained, thus supplementing not only the original volume, but also to some extent the Griffin *Bibliography of American Historical Societies.*[19]

Much material of value for historical purposes is published in the cognate fields of economics, sociology, political science, literature, biography, travel, etc. The indexes which have been described cover a great many of the periodicals containing such matter, and the investigator should keep in mind the importance of an intelligent use of subject entries. Legal studies are often of very great value for the historian, and for the law journals there exist special indexes. The chief of these are the *Index to Legal Periodical Literature*, in four volumes, covering the years prior to 1922, and the *Index to Legal Periodicals and Law Library Journal*, begun as a quarterly in 1908. The latter is the basis of a series of annual cumulations, which since 1922 form continuation volumes of the work first mentioned. A volume is projected cumulating entries for each three-year period.[20]

Much more than an index of articles is *Social Science Abstracts*, the first number of which appeared in February, 1929. This monthly is the product of some fifteen hundred coöperating scholars who systematically examine the current issues of more than forty-five hundred periodicals, in thirty-five languages, and prepare brief summaries of the significant articles. About 20,000 of these abstracts are published annually, in carefully classified order, and an extra number of the publication is issued at the end of the year containing a complete index.

It often becomes important to ascertain where files of periodicals may be found, since no library can be expected to contain

[19] See page 41.
[20] An excellent explanation of legal bibliography and methods of research in law is given in Spahr and Swenson, *Methods and Status of Scientific Research*, ch. IX.

all of those mentioned in a work like *Social Science Abstracts*. For this purpose coöperative catalogues are sometimes issued by groups of libraries in the same neighborhood, section, or even larger area. The most comprehensive publication of this kind is the *Union List of Serials in Libraries of the United States and Canada*, prepared by Winifred Gregory, and published in 1927.[21]

iii. GUIDES TO NEWSPAPERS

The contents of newspapers do not lend themselves to the same type of indexing that is feasible for magazines. A few papers have attempted indexes of their own issues, notably the *New York Daily Tribune*, for which there is an *Index* in 31 volumes, running from 1875 to 1906, and the *New York Times*, the *Index* of which was begun in 1913. In general, in using newspapers it is necessary for the investigator to ascertain what files exist for the locality and period involved in his study, and then to run through these files with little more clue to what may be found in them than the dates of important events. Most of the aids in the use of newspapers take the form of checklists of the papers in particular collections. Many of the larger libraries publish such lists.[22] The most extensive guide so far undertaken is that by Brigham, mentioned in the bibliography.

The most important general collection of newspapers in the United States is that in the Library of Congress, and the Division of Bibliography has issued a number of bulletins dealing with its own files and important ones elsewhere. The *Check-List of American Newspapers in the Library of Congress* is an example of its publications of this kind. There is need of a revision of this list, as it was published in 1901. The student may safely assume, however, that the files of the most important papers have been kept complete since that date.

[21] For bibliography of union lists see Mudge, *op. cit.*
[22] An exception to the rule about indexes to newspapers is found in the case of the California State Library, at Sacramento, which has a collection of some 8,000 volumes of newspapers, some running back to 1846, for which a card index has been made, containing 2,000,000 entries.

iv. GUIDES TO UNITED STATES GOVERNMENT DOCUMENTS

The publications of the United States Government form one of the classes of material most used by historical workers. They are so varied in character that it is difficult to carry in mind much information about them except that which is impressed upon the memory by constant use. Beyond a few simple directions, therefore, the best advice is to have at hand some reference work to which one may turn as occasion arises. The section on Government Documents in Mudge, *New Guide*, is compact and inclusive. Those who must make much use of documents should study carefully Edith F. Clarke's *Guide to the Use of United States Government Documents*.

The records of the Congresses which preceded the adoption of the Constitution have been republished in recent years, under the able editorship of Worthington C. Ford and Gaillard Hunt, with the title *Journals of the Continental Congresses*.

The record of the debates in Congress since 1789 has been printed under various titles. The debates from 1789 to 1824 are known as the *Annals of Congress;* the volumes for the years 1824–1837 are called the *Register of Debates in Congress;* the *Congressional Globe*, which overlaps the *Register*, begins in 1834 and carries the debates to 1873; since which time the name *Congressional Record* has been in use. All but the last were published as private enterprises sanctioned by the Government; the Government itself has published the *Record*, which in many ways improves upon its predecessors. Beginning with the *Register*, the record of a session of Congress is called a Volume, although often bound in a number of units, called Parts. Each Volume is indexed, but the subject entries are inadequate.

The Senate held secret sessions during the early years, and the printed records of its proceedings are most meager. The deficiency is supplied to a degree by the diaries of certain members. For the first two years one is available, kept by William Maclay of Pennsylvania, while for the early years of the nineteenth century that of William Plumer of New Hampshire fills a similar gap. Both of these diaries were published in comparatively recent times.[23]

In tracing the history of legislation, it is necessary in the earlier period to follow not only the debates in the two houses, but the *Journals* in which are preserved the official records of motions, votes, and other steps in parliamentary procedure. Since the publication of the *Record* began, the *Journals* have lost much of their significance.

The index to the *Record* includes a History of Bills and Resolutions on which there was action during the session, and in this every stage of the progress of each bill is given, together with the numbers of any reports or documents relating to it. In the early days acts as passed were printed in appendices in the volumes of the *Annals*, etc., but unfortunately for the historian, bills as originally presented or reported from committee are seldom incorporated either into the *Journals* or the debates. Great bundles of the printed sheets on which they came before the Houses are piled away in almost inaccessible places in Washington. The proceedings preserve the record of amendments, and the essence of the original proposals is usually evident on examination of the debates and the acts as passed.[24]

In later years the acts of each session have been published as passed in the temporary forms called Slip Laws and Pamphlet or Session Laws. All the laws passed by a Congress (covering the biennium) are collected into one volume, under the title *Statutes at Large*. As time passes and other legislation is enacted, some of these become obsolete or are modified, so that new publications become necessary, containing the general and permanent statutes in force.[25] These revisions are indispensable, of course, for the legal practitioner, but for the historian the original statutes, even if amended or repealed, are of equal or

[23] *Journal of William Maclay, United States Senator from Pennsylvania, 1789–1791*, edited by Edgar S. Maclay.

William Plumer's Memorandum of Proceedings in the United States Senate, 1803–1807, edited by Everett Somerville Brown.

[24] See Clarke, *op. cit.*, 130 *et seq.*, for fuller directions for tracing legislation.

[25] Spahr and Swenson, *op. cit.*, 183 *et seq.*, discuss the various forms in which revisions of statutes are published.

even greater importance, making the *Statutes at Large* invaluable.

Supplementing the *Journals* and debates are the *Reports of Committees* of Senate and House. Embodied in these is much documentary material collected by the committees because of its bearing on proposed legislation. This material is often of very great historical value. Another vast mass of material is contained in the *Documents*, which are for the most part publications emanating from executive departments or officials. They cover a very wide range of subjects.

Save for their voluminous character, there is little difficulty in following congressional debates if the dates when they began are known approximately. A brief examination of a volume of the *Annals*, *Globe*, or *Record* will show how they must be used. Helpful, however, are the comprehensive Tables of Contents of the Debates, Statutes, and Court Reports prepared by Church and Smith.[26]

The House and Senate *Journals* are also easily used. But to find data on a given topic in the documents is a very different matter. Much documentary matter was printed in appendices in the *Annals*, *Debates*, and *Globe*. At the end of the first generation under the Constitution, many documents were gathered into a series of *American State Papers*, which contained groups of volumes on *Foreign Relations*, *Military Affairs*, *Public Lands*, *Finance*, etc. Since then an elaborate and intricate system of reports has developed, which is well calculated (although not by design) to bury data beyond recovery.

Nearly every important administrative official makes an annual report, and many of these are printed, but the functions of these officials are transferred sometimes from one department to another, and other events occur which render it difficult to follow the records. For example, from 1832 to 1849 the report of the Commissioner of Indian Affairs was a part of the report

[26] Alonzo Webster Church and Henry H. Smith, *Tables Showing the Contents of the Several Volumes Comprising the Annals of Congress, Congressional Debates, Congressional Globe, Congressional Record, Statutes at Large, United States Supreme Court Reports . . . Arranged by Years and Congresses.*

of the Secretary of War, while after 1849 the Commissioner was transferred to the Interior Department and his report became a part of the annual statement of its head.[27]

From time to time documents of special classes have been collected and published. These compilations are often assigned places in the documents. As illustrations may be mentioned the compilations of C. J. Kappler, *Indian Affairs, Laws, and Treaties*, published in 1902 (57 Cong., 1 sess., *Sen. Doc. 452*); Thomas Donaldson, *The Public Domain* (47 Cong., 2 sess., *H. Misc. Doc. 45, Pt. 4*); James D. Richardson, *Messages and Papers of the Presidents* (53 Cong., 2 sess., *H. Misc. Doc. 40*); and William M. Malloy, *Treaties, Conventions, International Acts, Protocols and Agreements between the United States of America and Other Powers* (61 Cong., 2 sess., *Sen. Doc. 357*).[28]

A further illustration, showing the unexpected kinds of matter which government documents may contain, is found in the fact that the American Historical Association was incorporated by Congress in 1889, as a subsidiary of the Smithsonian Institution, to which it is required by the act of incorporation to make an annual report. The Institution in turn transmits the report to Congress, and it is then printed as a House Document. The *Report* for the year 1896, to take one at random, is placed thus in the document series: 54 Cong., 2 sess., *H. Doc. 353, Pts. 1 and 2.*

The search for such compilations is simplified by the fact that most libraries catalogue them separately. Many of them are published with what are called Plain Titles, as well as with the designation indicating their place in the documents—that is, with the same kind of title page that is found in ordinary books. The American Historical Association *Reports* have this dual form. Nevertheless, without some kind of comprehensive index the investigator would often be bewildered beyond hope.

---

[27] Note the recent transfer of the Commissioner for Prohibition from the Treasury Department to that of the Attorney General.

[28] This is properly the designation of volumes I and II of Malloy's work, which were issued in 1910. A supplement was published in 1913, which is designated thus: 62 Cong., 2 sess., *Sen. Doc. 1063;* while a third volume was issued as *Sen. Doc. 348* of the 4th session of the 67th Congress.

The first attempt in the direction of such an index was made by Benjamin Perley Poore, acting for the government, which published in 1885 the product of his labors under the title *Descriptive Catalogue of the Government Publications of the United States, September 5, 1774–March 4, 1881* (48 Cong., 2 sess., *Sen. Misc. Doc. 67*). The entries in this work are in chronological order, and include in each case an abstract of the document and information as to where it is to be found—that is, number, etc. The whole is indexed by authors, titles, and dates, but the index is inadequate for want of subject entries.

The deficiencies of Poore's index render valuable the second part of the *Tables of and Annotated Index to the Congressional Series of United States Public Documents*, a work published by the Superintendent of Documents in 1902.[29] Part II (the *Annotated Index*) is a "minute alphabetical subject index" of the Congressional series of documents from the Fifteenth Congress to the Fifty-second. Its chief limitation is the failure to include documents outside of the Congressional series.

More carefully planned and executed than Poore's *Catalogue* is the compilation, in two volumes, by John G. Ames, entitled *Comprehensive Index to the Publications of the United States Government, 1881–1893* (58 Cong., 2 sess., *H. Doc. 754*). Published in 1905, it bridges the gap between Poore's *Catalogue* and the comprehensive index prepared periodically by the Superintendent of Documents for publications issued since March 4, 1893. The full title of this last is *Catalogue of the Public Documents of Congress and of all Departments of the Government of the United States*. The first volume was issued in 1896, and each of the subsequent volumes covers the period of one Congress—two years.

This "Doc. Cat.," as it is commonly called, appears in primary form as the *Monthly Catalogue of United States Public Documents*, which affords a current list of all government publications. One year's issues (July to June) form a volume,

---

[29] The *Tables* which compose the first part of this work have been superseded by the *Checklist* mentioned below.

which is provided when completed with a detailed author and subject index. These annual volumes are superseded when the complete and permanent biennial volumes come out. These have elaborate indexes.

The Poore, Ames, and *Document Catalogue* in its two forms (with the *Annotated Index* to supplement Poore) taken collectively cover a large part of the field of Federal Documents. In addition there is a table which includes in one alphabet "an approximately complete checklist of all public documents issued by the United States government during the first century and a quarter of its history." This work is the *Checklist of United States Public Documents, 1789–1909*. The first volume, now in a third edition, covers the *American State Papers*, Congressional documents from the Fifteenth to the Sixtieth Congress, and department publications arranged alphabetically by authors. The second volume, not yet completed, will be an index.

A few indexes have been prepared for documents relating to special subjects. One of these, by Adelaide R. Hasse, is the *Index to United States Documents Relating to Foreign Affairs, 1828–1861*. The work bridges the gap between the matter published in the *American State Papers*, which are indexed, and the beginning, in 1861, of the annual indexed volumes of *Diplomatic Correspondence*. For these last there is a general index to 1899. Miss Hasse's *Index* is not a government publication, but was prepared under the patronage of the Carnegie Institution. As time passes more and more work of this type is likely to be done by government agencies or private organizations and endowments.

V. GUIDES TO GOVERNMENT ARCHIVES

The Carnegie Institution has also promoted the preparation of a series of guides to archival materials relating to American history. The first of these volumes, by Claude Halstead Van Tyne and Walter G. Leland, was published in 1907, under the title *Guide to the Archives of the Government of the United States in Washington*. It was intended, of course, to assist investigators who desired to make use of unpublished official papers. The scattered condition of these papers (for want of an archives building, for which the American Historical Association has long labored with scant success) makes the *Guide* even more useful than it would otherwise be.

Guides to the Cuban and Spanish archives were issued in this same year (1907), and by the assignment of different countries to different experts, the preparation of other volumes was so hastened that in less than a decade some sixteen had been published. The series covers the principal depositories in Great Britain, Germany, Austria, Switzerland, Russia, Italy, Spain, Canada, and Mexico, as well as the United States. For the last, besides the volume by Van Tyne and Leland, there is one on Protestant Church archives, one on territorial papers in Washington, and one on transcripts of Spanish documents in American libraries.[30]

Another guide, which really belongs in the same series, lists manuscripts on American history in European libraries.[31]

vi. GENERAL AND MISCELLANEOUS GUIDES

There are several helpful lists and calendars which for want of a more logical place will be mentioned here. Most of them are publications of the Library of Congress. The Division of Manuscripts issued in 1918 a *Handbook of Manuscripts in the Library of Congress*, with the object of presenting "the whole resources of the division in a comprehensive way." It contains a description of the origin, scope, form, period, and contents of each of the collections, and is indexed.

The same division is constantly issuing calendars and lists of papers of statesmen in its possession, and has published separate bulletins on the papers of Crittenden, Franklin, Monroe, Pierce, Van Buren, Washington, and many others.

In 1916 the division sent a questionnaire to 232 historical

[30] For a complete list of these guides, see Mudge, *op. cit.*
[31] David M. Matteson, *List of Manuscripts Concerning American History Preserved in European Libraries and Noted in Their Published Catalogues and Similar Printed Lists.*

societies, universities, and libraries requesting information concerning the location of papers of Americans prominent in civil, religious, and military affairs. The returns (from 86 institutions) were printed in 1918 under the title *Checklist of Collections of Personal Papers in Historical Societies, Universities, and Public Libraries and Other Learned Institutions in the United States.* The data are presented in three forms: (1) in the alphabetical order of the names of the persons; (2) in a chronological table; and (3) under the names of the institutions where the papers are held. Although the information is so incomplete, the *Checklist* is extremely valuable and represents effort of a type which it is to be hoped will be carried out much more thoroughly in the future.

Some conception of the scope of the publications of the Division of Bibliography can be formed from the following partial list of subjects on which bibliographies have been compiled and printed:

> Alaska, Amendments to the Constitution, Bank of the United States, Cabinet, Canals and Railways, Canadian Reciprocity, Cartularies, Child Labor, Civil War, Colonization, Conservation, Constitution, Consular Service, Cuba, Danish West Indies, Eight-hour Movement, Embargoes, Far East, French Alliance, Genealogy, Germans in the United States, Hawaii, Immigration, Impeachments, Initiative and Referendum, International Arbitration, International Law, International Politics, Labor, Lincolniana, Maps (numerous classes in separate bulletins of the Maps and Manuscript Division), Money, Monroe Doctrine, Municipal Government, Negroes, Newspapers (several), Philippines (several), Political Parties, Porto Rico, Postal Savings Banks, Primary Elections, Proportional Representation, Railroads, Reciprocity, Samoa and Guam, Short Ballot, Senators (popular election), Supreme Court, Tariff, Treaty-making Power, Trusts, Virginia Company, World War (several), etc.

A means of checking the entries in any library catalogue relating to the publications of the Library of Congress is afforded by its bulletin on *Publications Issued . . . since 1897* (published in 1920). Much information of bibliographical value, in addition to what has been given here, may be obtained by examining this volume. For recent additions to the map and manuscript collections, and for publications since 1920, one must resort to the *Annual Report of the Librarian of Congress*, or to the separate pamphlets listing accessions issued from time to time by the respective divisions. They may be found by checking through the successive issues of the "Doc. Cat."

vii. GUIDES SPECIFICALLY FOR AMERICAN HISTORY

For many years there was no comprehensive index for the numerous periodicals published by national, sectional, state, and local historical societies. The articles in only the more important of these periodicals are included in the general indexes, and no good index for them as a class existed until the publication of A. P. C. Griffin's *Bibliography of American Historical Societies*. This work, in its revised form, fills the second volume of the American Historical Association *Report* for 1905. It lists national societies in one alphabet, while local societies are placed in alphabetical order under their respective states. Under each society appears the complete table of contents of every number of its periodical publications. The whole is well indexed by authors and subjects.

Some of the periodical indexes already mentioned serve to a limited extent as supplements to Griffin's *Bibliography*,[32] but its work is continued most effectively in the series of annual volumes known as *Writings on American History*. This series has had a checkered career, under several editors and publishers. It made its début in 1904, under the auspices of Princeton University, in the shape of an exhaustive bibliography of books and articles on United States history published during the year 1902. In 1905 the enterprise was taken over by the Carnegie Institution, which brought out the volume for the year 1903. Three years then elapsed before arrangements could be made for continuing the work, but at length a guarantee fund was raised, and in 1908 a third volume was issued, covering the publications of 1906.

[32] See page 3?

This volume was prepared under the editorial direction of Grace Gardner Griffin, who from that time became responsible for the annual issues. The publication is invaluable but has never paid its way. The problem of financing it has been continuous, and its existence precarious in consequence. It has been published in turn by the Macmillan Company, the Government, the Yale University Press, and again by the Government, as a part of the American Historical Association *Annual Report*.

Meanwhile the scope and value of the work have been extended and enhanced. From the outset it was intended to be exhaustive for the United States and full for British America. Beginning with the issue for 1906, the editors aimed to include all writings on the United States and British America published in the United States, British America, or Europe, whether in the form of books, pamphlets, or periodical articles. The index of each volume guides the student to all entries of interest to him, but the necessity of examining so many separate indexes is a drawback. For publications of the years covered by the *Writings* there is hardly any need of other indexes.

For books on local history the best guide for the period previous to the inception of the *Writings* is the work by Thomas L. Bradford, *Bibliographer's Manual of American History, Containing an Account of all State, Territory, Town and County Histories Relating to the United States of North America*. This work, in five volumes, was published during the years 1907–1910, and has an exhaustive index by titles and states. It is, however, none too accurate.

viii. GUIDES TO STATE MATERIALS

It is not possible within reasonable space limits to discuss the various aids which have been published to assist research in state and local history as fully as the more general aspects of research have been presented. The student whose subject relates to the history of a particular state or region must ascertain just what local historical agencies have published that will aid him. A difficulty arises at this point from the fact that information about some classes of matter for the history of a particular locality may be contained, not in any publication by that state, but in some bibliography or checklist issued by the Library of Congress, or even by a local library in a remote locality.

It may become necessary to consult the proper officials by mail or in person. It is safe to say, however, that a very trustworthy list of all bibliographical publications of the last quarter century relating to the history of any state may be compiled by anyone who has access to a complete file of the *Writings on American History*. Nor should the uses to which other works already described may be put, be overlooked. Bradford's *Manual*, Griffin's *Bibliography*, the Library of Congress *Checklist of Personal Papers*, the *Readers' Guide*, and other aids, might be mentioned again in this connection. Many publications of the Federal Government bear upon local history, in such aspects as settlement, economic, social, and political development, Indian relations, etc., and for these the aids already described should be used.

The bibliography in this manual contains a section in which are listed representative bibliographies for state history. There are a few guides to local materials which may be mentioned here because their scope is so inclusive as to make them generally valuable to students of local history. One of these, prepared by Adelaide R. Hasse, is the *Index of Economic Material in Documents of the States*. This work, sponsored by the Carnegie Institution, includes volumes for California, Delaware, Illinois, Kentucky, Maine, Massachusetts, New Hampshire, New Jersey, New York, Ohio, Pennsylvania, Rhode Island, and Vermont. In each instance the *Index* covers the years of statehood, and deals only with the printed reports of administrative officers, legislative committees, special commissions, and governors' messages.

Supplementing the Hasse *Index*, and including more states and other classes of documents, is Richard R. Bowker's *State Publications*, in four volumes. This is a provisional checklist, valuable for state materials antedating the issue of the several volumes; the volume for the New England states appeared in 1899, while that on the states of the South came ten years later. Soon after the appearance of the final volume, the Division of Documents of the Library of Congress began to issue (1910) a *Monthly Checklist of State Publications*.

A helpful list of bibliographies of documents published by states is given in James R. Childs, *An Account of Government Document Bibliography*.[33]

The four guides mentioned are limited almost exclusively to government publications, state or Federal. In tracing publications of other kinds bearing on state history, it is often helpful to know what organizations or agencies exist in a particular state which may have issued them. A list of most of these is given in the *Handbook of Learned Societies and Institutions*, which is another of the many contributions of the Carnegie Institution to the tools of scholarship. It gives (among other data) the name, address, purpose, and publications of each organization, and while the information is in some respects out of date, the book having been published in 1908, it still gives valuable clues as to paths of inquiry which may be pursued further. Thus one who learned from the *Handbook* that a certain historical society had published a calendar of manuscripts or list of newspapers would be led to inquire whether later lists of the same nature had been issued by the society; moreover the information in the *Handbook* would suggest whether the inquiry should be pursued by correspondence with officials or by examination of the later issues of some serial publication of the society.

Much information relating to the archives of the states has been published from time to time in the *Annual Reports* of the American Historical Association. This information is most readily accessible through the general index, which forms a part of the *Report* for 1914. For the later volumes the separate indexes, or the annual volumes of *Writings on American History*, must be consulted.

[33] Pages 14–22.

There is a section in Larned's *Literature of American History* in which are described the chief published collections of sources for state history.[34] Although old it is still useful. Valuable suggestions of a similar kind are given in the Channing, Hart, and Turner *Guide*.[35] Some additional items are included in the bibliography at the close of this manual.

e. *The Expansion of the Bibliography File: the Relation of the Tentative and Final Bibliographies*

As the number of slips with bibliographical data increases, the plan of filing will doubtless need to be expanded to take care of them. One division may well be devoted to "Newspapers," and another to "Articles in Periodicals, Annuals, and Publications of Learned Societies." Another will probably be required for "Government Publications," with perhaps such subdivisions as Federal, State, and Local, or Municipal. Before filing slips in any of these classes appropriate topical headings should be written at the top of each. Within each class or subdivision an alphabetical order should be observed in filing. Thus in the periodical list an article by Bassett would go under B and one by Esarey under E. This plan will scatter the references to articles by different writers in the same magazine, and bring together those by the same writer in different periodicals. Newspaper items, on the contrary, should be collected under the name of the paper, all slips referring to the *New York Times* or *Public Opinion*, for example, being brought together regardless of authors or topics. The topical headings suggest a convenient order of arrangement under the name of the paper; and under each topic, if the slips are numerous, a chronological order of arrangement will usually be best. A series of cross references may be used to bring together items in different papers on the same topic.

The reason for this seemingly arbitrary difference in the methods of handling newspaper and periodical matter will

[34] Pages 7–13.   [35] Pages 132–150.

appear in the discussion of the form for the final bibliography.[36] As will be apparent later, the topical segregation of periodical matter is taken care of in the filing of notes on subject-matter.[37]

As the tentative bibliography expands, it should gradually take on its final form and content, leaving at last little more to be done than to transcribe it.

4. NOTE-TAKING

It is not to be understood that the bibliography must be completed before the study of subject-matter and the taking of notes are begun. On the contrary, the examination of material and note-taking will naturally and most economically accompany the collection of items for the bibliography; and new items will probably be found and used down to the very moment of completing the final revision of the study. Indeed, as knowledge of the subject grows the perspective will improve, and the quest for material needed to make the study complete will be the more intelligently directed. The ability to discriminate between the relevant and the irrelevant in the tentative bibliography will also increase, so that the final form may be prepared with good judgment.

a. *What to Take: Quotations and Condensations*

During the process of becoming familiar with the background history which serves as the setting for the theme, one chief purpose of reading is to make sure of the knowledge which is a part of the preliminary equipment for the special undertaking. Any notes which may be taken at this stage are mainly auxiliary to this purpose. The background facts may be obtained from secondary treatises, and so far as notes of dates, outlines of events, or other matter, will aid the memory, they should be taken. But it is assumed that the intelligent reader of a monograph, as well as the writer, is acquainted with the general facts

[36] See page 125.   [37] See pages 54–55.

set forth in standard secondary treatises, and the writer will owe him no apology for treating such data as a common stock of knowledge.

To illustrate: while reading Sparks, *National Development*, one might, to aid the memory, make a memorandum of the date of President Arthur's accession; but in writing on "President Arthur and Civil Service Reform" it would be absurd to cite Sparks, or anyone else, as authority for this date.

It does not follow that a general history is never to be cited. It is quite possible that the writer of such a work expresses an opinion upon some phase of the subject under investigation. An opinion or judgment of such an author is not a background fact, but a specific item, which the monograph writer may wish to contrast or compare with the conclusions of other writers, not excepting himself. In case of such use, a citation of the place where such expression of opinion occurs will have to be given. In other words, facts relating to one's particular subject must be dealt with, both in taking notes and in writing the study, quite differently from background facts.

The distinction between these two classes of data should be kept constantly in mind, in order that proper notes may be made of those facts or statements for which authority must be cited when the monograph is written. This is not always easy, because there are facts which serve as links between the general and the special, and partake of the nature of both; and it is often difficult to decide how to treat them. The passage of the Pendleton Act is a well known fact of general history, and at the same time it is an outstanding fact in the history of civil service reform under Arthur. Should the dates of passage of the bill by House and Senate be regarded as general or specific facts? Only common sense can answer such questions. If a monograph writer decides to cite authority in a matter of this kind, he should cite the best, *i.e.*, the record of the proceedings in Congress, rather than a general history.

The application of these reflections to the question of note-taking is that facts which pertain to the particular theme, as contradistinguished from those of general history, should be made note of and filed in the form in which they will be most useful when the investigator is ready to write his monograph.

Beginning with background reading, one proceeds to works relating more specifically to one's theme, selecting first those which appear most valuable for the purpose, and turning more and more to sources as one becomes aware of the phases of the theme which permit or demand original treatment.

What should be taken in notes depends very greatly upon the use to which it is anticipated the matter will be put. In practice the chief difficulty is to anticipate the use with accuracy; it may be but vaguely defined at the outset, and as it becomes clearer it may show that the earlier notes are not in satisfactory form. During the early stages of an investigation, it often happens that the notes taken are too inclusive. The fear of omitting something which may be needed later is quite likely to produce this result. This is perhaps better than the mistake of failing to note something which is afterwards found to be essential. Both errors are wasteful of time and should be avoided as far as possible.

A warning is not out of place against the danger of allowing one's attention to be distracted by interesting items not related to one's theme. The novice who engages in the examination of old newspapers is peculiarly susceptible to this temptation, and unless he steels himself against it, he is likely to discover that he has wasted much precious time. Another golden mean which must be assiduously sought is the course which runs between too great a dependence upon the memory, on the one hand, and the taking of unnecessarily voluminous notes on the other.

Like the reporter's scent for news, the historian's instinct for data really pertinent to his study develops through use. The beginner will often discover that the notes which he took in the earlier stages of a study must be recast, supplemented, or boiled down. This labor will be minimized if the loose-leaf system, as explained below, is used, and a separate slip made for each item.

While the use which it is expected will be made of the matter is always the best guide in taking notes, the character of the document from which they are taken has something to do with their form. Presumably few if any are needed on background reading. A monograph on a topic closely related to that in hand may require an abstract, in which conclusions, points of view, and evidence especially stressed, are noted. In making such an abstract the investigator may appropriately employ any system of abbreviations or short cuts which will be intelligible to him, except where he makes actual quotations.

Only the most significant views or statements need be quoted as a rule, although it may be necessary sometimes to copy the whole of an important document. Whenever a passage is quoted it must be inclosed in quotation marks and the utmost pains must be taken to reproduce *exactly* the words, spelling, punctuation, capitalization, etc., of the original. If there are errors, the investigator must not correct them, but should indicate that he has followed the original by inserting in brackets, immediately following the error, the Latin word *sic*, thus: [sic]. Brackets should be used in every case where one interpolates words of one's own within quotations.

There is frequently need of interpolations, as an expression may occur in the quotation which refers to something which precedes the quoted words in the original, and would not be intelligible without explanatory comment. Suppose that one wishes to quote a passage concerning Washington's military leadership and his name does not appear in the part quoted. In such a case the name should be supplied in the following way: "This great captain [George Washington] was one of the ablest generals of the eighteenth century." *Do not make the mistake of using parentheses () instead of brackets [] for this purpose.* The former cannot be distinguished from the quoted portion of the passage.

If it is desired to omit certain words within a quoted passage, an omission is indicated by three periods at the point where the words are left out. If the words would have ended a sentence, the omission is indicated by four periods, thus. . . .

These suggestions about quoted passages are equally applicable in note-taking and in using quotations in a monograph. If not heeded when notes are taken, there will be doubt when the moment comes to use the quotation, and time will be wasted in referring to the source to check the accuracy of the copy.

Returning to the relation between the character of a document and the notes to be taken: an abstract of the whole may be needed, with an exact quotation of the central part. Speeches and court decisions may usually be handled in this way. Similarly, in the case of a bill or statute, one section may contain all that need be copied verbatim, the other sections being designated merely by captions indicating their nature. It is almost impossible, however, to paraphrase statements made in technical language, such as is used in laws, constitutions, and court decisions, without losing some of the essential meaning or doing violence to it. The further caution is needed that especial care must be taken, in all cases where passages are quoted, not to divorce them from their context in such a way that they will seem to mean what the document as a whole, or its author, does not mean. The abstract, condensation, or quotation must be so made that the meaning of the original is preserved with exactitude.

In making abstracts, condensations, or summaries, comments often occur to the student which he desires to jot down at the proper point in the notes. Care is needed to distinguish these comments from the notes on what has been read. Perhaps the best device for effecting this is to form the habit of inclosing one's own comment in brackets, just as if the notes consisted entirely of quoted matter.

A type of note-taking which presents especial difficulty to the novice is that in which numerous speeches are made on the same subject, as for example in a Congressional debate on a matter of great public interest, such as the Compromise of 1850. The mere mass of matter is often almost terrifying, because of the time that would be required to sift it carefully. It is usually not very difficult to discover the few chief speakers on each side, and it is generally true that the other speakers add very little to the arguments of these leaders. This fact makes it feasible to examine a few speeches intensively, giving the rest only a cursory inspection to make sure that nothing of significance is overlooked. This method may be adapted to many kinds of investigation where the mass of material seems, at first glance, to be ominously large.

When one has a definite idea of the use which will be made of the notes on a book, monograph, article, or speech, they may be broken into convenient units for distribution in the appropriate topical divisions of the note file. This is made possible by the use of the system described in the following section.

b. *The Loose-Leaf System*

It is a fundamental rule of modern practice in note-taking that each item must be entered on a separate slip of paper. The older historians were hampered by lack of this simple mechanical device. When George Bancroft began to take notes, about a century ago, preparatory to writing his *History of the United States*, he could think of no better plan for organizing them than to provide himself with a number of bound volumes of blank paper, one for each year, with a page for each day. As he read he entered his notes of events on the pages corresponding to the dates of their occurrence, thus giving a chronological organization to the whole mass of notes. The limitations of this method, and the burden which it threw upon the author's powers of memory, account for some of the faults in Bancroft's *History;* yet a half-century later writers were still recording notes in bound books, and laboriously compiling indexes, when the note-taking was completed, as the only means by which all notes bearing upon the same topics could be brought into view at one time.

When during the 1880's some of the leading libraries discarded the printed and bound catalogues which made impossible the insertion of accessions in their proper alphabetical position, and adopted instead the present type of card catalogue, which is always up to date, historical writers, as well as others, promptly adapted the new method to their needs, and thus the loose-leaf system came into use for note-taking.

Briefly stated, the merit of the method consists in the facility with which notes on any phase of a subject, although taken at random, are brought into actual physical contact. The benefits of the system will not be obtained in full unless one is skillful in breaking notes into the convenient units referred to in the preceding section. To say that only one item should be entered on a slip is easy, but it is not so easy to determine what one item is. The terms "unit" and "item" as used here have the same meaning, but the practical question remains, whether an abstract of a book, speech, or document is one item or many. It can only be answered that the same abstract may, for one purpose, be a single item, while for another purpose it may constitute two or more. A note taken while the prospective use is still uncertain will often include several items, as will be judged later, so that parts may have to be recopied and distributed in the appropriate places, or cross-reference slips will have to be made and placed in each of these places, referring to the inclusive item.

c. *Use of Headings and Citations*

When bibliography notes were being considered, allusion was made to the variety of choices in the matter of the sizes and kinds of cards or slips for use in note-taking. It was then suggested that there were advantages in using the same kind of paper for both bibliography and notes, since both could then be filed in the same cabinet. It cannot be expected that workers will agree in their preferences in such matters, and there is no need of agreement. Each person must determine his preference by his own experiments.

The present writer uses a filing cabinet with drawers wide and deep enough to receive an ordinary sheet of typewriter paper (8½ x 11 inches)—the same type of cabinet that is used in business offices to contain letters from correspondents. This size affords room for the bodily insertion of manuscripts on full-sized sheets, pamphlets, and reprints or articles from journals. For note-taking, however, he uses half-size sheets (5½ x 8½). These are large enough to hold a good many words, and at the same time cheap enough to allow one to write only a line or two on a sheet without the pricks of conscience which attend wastefulness.

Whatever size sheets are chosen, certain data are essential on every note. The notes proper, consisting of abstracts or quotations or both, may run over on to a second page or more. But in addition to the notes there must always be given: (1) an exact citation of the source whence they were taken; and (2) a heading showing the contents of the note and affording a clue to the filing of the slip.

If more than one sheet is required for the note, the heading should be repeated in brief form at the top of each and the page or sheet numbered. There is no hard and fast rule as to where the citation shall be placed on the slip, but trouble will result if it is omitted entirely. The habit should be formed promptly of recording it with meticulous care. For this reason it is a good practice to place it on the sheet before anything else is written. The heading can be added whenever a suitable wording is thought of. The form of citation may be as brief as is consistent with positive indentification of the source of the information; and the citation should be repeated on the following sheets if more than one is required for the item. Otherwise, if a sheet becomes misplaced, difficulty may be experienced in restoring it to its proper position.

It frequently happens that a running summary of several pages of a book under examination can be placed on a single page of notes. It is well in that case to indicate the point in the notes at which the successive pages of the original begin by inclosing the page numbers in brackets at the point in the notes just preceding the abstract for that page. This makes it always possible to cite the exact page of the authority when making a citation in the process of writing the monograph.

The foregoing points may now be illustrated by the following form:

President Hayes and Civil Service

Sparks, <u>Nat</u>. <u>Dev</u>., 154–

Hayes championed reform from beginning of term. [155] Did not wait for Cong. to approp. money for C. S. Commission, but forbade govt. officials to levy camp. assess. [156] In this way aroused wrath of the politicians. [157] Reappointed James, reformer,

Pres. Hayes & C. S.–2.

Sparks.

as N. Y. postmaster. [158] Removed head of N. Y. customs office. [159] Led to contest with Stalwarts.

d. *Filing of Notes: Relation to Outline for Writing*

Loose-leaf notes, if skillfully broken into units and given proper headings, are self-indexing and easily filed according to subject. The obsolete method of using a bound book scattered notes on the same matter, but the loose-leaf system brings them together. As knowledge of the subject under investigation grows, its divisions and subdivisions should rise above the mental horizon and form at the same time a tentative outline for writing the monograph and a guide to the probable use to be made of each new fact added to the notes. This growing perception of the probable use to be made of the items suggests, as has been said, the proper units into which notes should be broken, and the net result of the whole process is that the scheme of note-taking and filing gradually approximates the outline which the writer will use as a guide in composing the essay. If, when he begins to write, his notes are arranged in the file in conformity with the outline of the monograph, the mechanics of his procedure may be said to approximate perfection.

If the sheets used for notes are 5½ x 8½ inches, it will be difficult to use guide cards in the filing cabinet. A convenient substitute will be found in the manila folders in common use in business office letter files. One edge of a folder of this kind stands a little higher than the other when in position in the cabinet, and affords space for words describing the contents. The bibliography slips, arranged in proper groups according to the subdivisions, with the items in each group alphabetized, may be placed in the first folder in the file, and other folders as needed may be used for the notes pertaining to each main division of the subject. An elaborate study may require separate folders for subdivisions, with some system of notation to distinguish subordinate divisions from the main ones. Using the Table of Contents of the present manual as an illustration, one might indorse the first folder thus: [38]

> I. The Gathering of Data:
>   1. Choosing a Subject

Coming to subdivision 3, with its subordinate parts, such a form as the following might be used for the heading:

> I. 3. The Tentative Bibliography:
>   a. Items from the Lib. Cat.

It would not be necessary to repeat the entire heading on every folder. In the above example, the words The Gathering of Data, instead of being repeated, are indicated by the numeral I.

It will now be apparent that while in the bibliography a number of articles by the same writer, published in the same or different magazines, would be brought together, the notes on each would be distributed in the file according to the topic with which each article dealt. This plan places the data of each kind just where it will best serve the writer's purpose.

The scheme of filing may be developed indefinitely and adapted to the needs of the student who continues his activity as writer or teacher of history. A course of lectures may be worked out and notes in any quantity whatever may be filed exactly according to the organization of the outline of lectures given to the class. As notes are added the outline may be expanded so that both may always be fully coördinated.

[38] These illustrations are for form only; the actual words would hardly fit any real case.

II. THE CRITICISM OF DATA

INTRODUCTION

Much historical writing has been done by authors who had a cause to serve, or, in less dignified phrase, an "ax to grind." They have written to promote the fortunes of a party or sect, to stimulate patriotism, or to inspire emulation of great characters. Other writers have chosen historical themes as fit subject-matter on which to exercise their literary skill. As a result there has been more or less distortion of facts, and what has passed for history has often been little more than "fiction agreed upon."

Perhaps there has never been a time when it has been wholly forgotten that the central purpose of history is to tell the *truth*, but historians have too often allowed prejudice, credulity, and passion to lead them astray. Then, too, the idea of what is required to establish the truth has undergone development. Until recent times many of the leading writers regarded *authority* (statements in Scripture, taken literally, or dogmas of the Church) as conclusive wherever it could be invoked. This attitude, while not wholly supplanted, has given way quite generally among intelligent students to the belief that facts can be ascertained and the truth established only by the examination of *evidence*. Here again there has been an evolution. Beginning with the idea that, with a proper application of the rules of evidence, the truth can be ascertained *absolutely*, historians have learned that the utmost they can hope for is to establish facts *beyond reasonable doubt*.

During the last hundred years, historical method has been much influenced by the progress of natural science. Historians have caught the scientific spirit and have sought to adapt the methods of science to their peculiar problems. Some have made efforts to discover and formulate the laws governing human actions, assuming that, as natural phenomena, they must be governed by such laws. But that type of problem has come to be regarded as too complex and inscrutable for the historian's tools, and in general they have accepted the more modest rôle of narrators and interpreters of *faits accomplis*, leaving to the newer sciences of sociology and psychology the investigation of the laws governing human conduct. Nevertheless, in their efforts to interpret the past, historians do not hesitate to appropriate the results obtained by these sciences, and in future will doubtless draw even more heavily upon them.

Historians have reached substantial agreement that their subject is not a science, in the sense at least in which chemistry and physics are sciences, because their procedure is necessarily different from that of scientists who employ the methods of *direct* observation. However, *the work of the historian, no less than that of the scientist, must rest upon reliable observation.* The difference in procedure is due to the fact that the historian usually does not make his own observations, and that those upon whose observations he must depend are often if not usually untrained observers. Historical method, strictly speaking, is a process *supplementary* to observation, a process by which the historian attempts to test the truthfulness of the reports of observations made by others.

Modern historians are scientists in the sense that they share the scientific spirit in seeking to apply critical principles as instruments in attaining trustworthy results, that is, in building up a body of dependable information. Although, unlike the other subjects mentioned, history is not a science of direct observation, it shares with them the use of hypothesis. Scientific method may be described as consisting essentially of three processes: observation, hypothesis, and experiment. The latter two are really only phases of the process of observation. A hypothesis is a tentative generalization or conclusion, resulting from observation, and used to guide further observation, in the light of which it is likely to be modified. The further observation often takes the form of experimentation, which may be described as controlled observation. The form of the experiment, moreover, is dictated by the hypothesis. All three processes are thus phases of systematized observation. Contrary to popular notions, the scientist does not proceed with his feet constantly upon the solid rock of ascertained fact. A part of the time he must be formulating and testing hypotheses or he could not proceed at all. Scientific thinking is always in advance of scientific knowledge, and leads the way to new truths.

In a similar way the historian examines his data and formulates hypotheses or tentative conclusions. These send him back, not to make new observations or experiments, but to find fresh evidence or to reëxamine old evidence, and this process is continued until, in the light of all obtainable evidence, the hypothesis is abandoned as untenable, established as true, or modified until it becomes a conclusion actually supported by the evidence.[1]

The purpose of the historian is to ascertain *facts*, which become the basis of all generalizations or conclusions (these being also facts of a higher order, serving to give history its meaning and value). But the raw materials with which the historian works are *statements*, and the first lesson which he must learn is that statements must not be mistaken for facts. They may be identical, but the identity cannot be taken for granted. His task is, if possible, to make such a use of statements that he will through them arrive at facts.

A statement is merely what some one has said about a matter, and there are many reasons why statements may not be wholly or even partially true. The maker may or may not have witnessed the event; he may have lied deliberately; he may have colored his report more or less unconsciously because of his own interests, sympathies, or prejudices; he may through ignorance, or some other type of incompetence, have been incapable of making an accurate observation and report of the matter in question.

[1] For an admirable presentation of the use of hypothesis in historical work, see Allen Johnson, *The Historian and Historical Evidence*, chap. VII.

In view of all these possibilities of error, it becomes the duty of the historian to doubt every statement until it has been critically tested. A proper examination will reveal the falsity of some statements, and the doubtfulness of others. Still others will emerge from the ordeal indorsed as probably true, or true beyond reasonable doubt.

The critical examination of statements involves two distinct processes (which the critic may learn to carry on simultaneously). The first is preliminary and preparatory, in that it affords the data which the second must employ, and is known as External (or Lower) Criticism. It examines *documents*—a term which here includes not only manuscripts but books, pamphlets, maps, etc.—with the aim of obtaining all possible information of any significance concerning their origin, and, if need be, of restoring the original form or wording. External criticism really begins with the collection of material, if one gathers data about origins at the same time. The comment in a trial bibliography that Fish, author of the monograph on *The Civil Service and the Patronage*, is a professor in the University of Wisconsin, illustrates the way in which some of the data for the critical process may be accumulated during the preparation of the bibliography.

Equipped with the results obtained by external criticism, Internal (or Higher) Criticism seeks to determine the *meaning* and *trustworthiness* of *statements* (not *documents*). Internal criticism is intended to yield, in effect, a sifted body of statements, classified according to the degree of probability which each possesses—a mass of information in which *facts* will stand out in clear relief, ready for use in a discriminating and truthful essay.

1. EXTERNAL CRITICISM

a. *Determination of the Circumstances Attending Production of the Document*

In one way or another documents often come to be regarded as what they are not. Sometimes forgeries gain acceptance, while other spurious documents result from errors of various kinds. It is obvious that the historian cannot judge of the trustworthiness of statements in a document unless he knows that the document itself is really what it purports or seems to be. The investigation of its origin may reveal that it is spurious.

i. INTERNAL ANALYSIS

The investigation of the origin of a document includes the effort to determine such facts as the identity of the author, his party, sect, race, and other group affiliations, and the time and place of writing. Without some data of these kinds internal criticism has little to work upon. The mere name of an author, however, is less significant than information of the other kinds, since it reveals nothing as to his bias or prejudice that is not evident on the face of the document. Internal evidence alone may afford much of the information which external criticism seeks. (Note that the terms "external" and "internal" as applied to criticism refer to *purpose*, not *method*. External criticism employs internal evidence, found by examining the document itself, while internal criticism often utilizes external evidence.)

In the issues of the *North American Review* during the year 1879 there appeared a series of extracts from the diary of "A Public Man" whose name remains unknown to this day. Internal evidence discloses that he "was a man of public distinction. He had been long in residence at Washington. His contacts with the leading personages at the Capitol were numerous. Though . . . a Northerner and a stanch Unionist, he was in touch with Southern leaders. He was recognized as a conservative and a lover of peace. . . . He had been a Whig; he was probably now a Republican and . . . a member of the Senate." [2] Such data are far more useful to the critic in judging of statements in the diary than the bare name of the writer could possibly be.

ii. COMPARISON WITH OTHER DOCUMENTS

If a writer's name can be ascertained, it usually brings in its train other desired facts about his characteristics and connec-

[2] Johnson, *op. cit.*, 59–60.

tions; hence external criticism very properly endeavors to ascertain the authorship in the case of documents where it is anonymous or uncertain. The critic who is most familiar with other documentary sources of the class to which an anonymous document belongs is the one who is best prepared to solve the problem of its authorship. He will find clues where the novice may see none (hence one reason for becoming thoroughly familiar with all sources bearing upon a theme).

Among the documents recording the story of the early exploration and settlement of Virginia there is one entitled "A Relatyon of the Discovery of our River, Made by Capt. Christopher Newport, and sincerely written and observed by a gentleman of the Colony." This document was first published in 1860, by the American Antiquarian Society.[3] The editor, Edward Everett Hale, did not identify the "gentleman of the Colony" who wrote it, but later scholars, more familiar with contemporary materials, think that the author was Captain Gabriel Archer, the Recorder of the Colony. The evidence is as follows:

The "Relatyon" informs us that Captain Newport took with him five "gentlemen, four maryners, and fourteen saylors," making a party of twenty-four, all of whose names are recorded in the document. As it is altogether unlikely that a "maryner" or "saylor" wrote the account, attention is at once directed to the five gentlemen. Of these, three seem more likely than the others to have been the author. One of these three was Robert Tyndal, who prepared the first map of the country; another is Gabriel Archer, whose duty as Recorder might be regarded as making it his task *ex officio* to set down the facts about the expedition; the third is John Smith, known as the most indefatigable of the writers on the beginnings of the colony. Smith is eliminated, however, as soon as the critic realizes that a brief account of this same journey appears in his "True Relation," an account sufficiently different from the anonymous "Relatyon" to prove that it is not from the same hand.

[3] *Archæologia Americana*, IV, 40–65.

Now it happens that when this party was in the neighborhood of the falls of James River, they discovered that the Indians of that region were hostile to those on Chesapeake Bay. This fact suggested a bid for their friendship, on the basis of common enmity to the Chesapeake tribes. The passage in the "Relatyon" reads:

> Also we perceived the Chessipian to be an enemye generally to all thes kyngdomes; upon which I tooke occasion to signifye our displeasure with them also; making it knowne that we refused to plant in their countrys; that we had warres with them also, shewing hurts scarce whole, received by [from] them. . . .

The use of the pronoun I in this passage strongly suggests that the writer showed wounds which he had himself received. Yet a critic's attention would hardly be arrested by the passage unless his knowledge of other documents enabled him to correlate this statement with them. One of these other documents bears the title "Observations gathered out of a Discourse of the Plantation of the Southerne Colonie in Virginia by the English, 1606." [4] The author was "that Honorable Gentleman, Master George Percy." In this document, commonly called "Percy's Discourse," occurs the following passage descriptive of events which took place several days before the journey up the James River under Newport:

> April 26. About foure a clocke in the morning, wee descried the Land of Virginia. The same day wee entred into the Bay of Chesupioc. . . . There we landed and discovered a little way. . . . At night, when we were going aboard, there came the Savages creeping upon all foure, from the Hills, like Beares, with their Bowes in their mouthes, charged us very desperately in the faces, hurt Captaine Gabrill Archer in both his hands, and a sayler in two places of the body very dangerous. . . .

Smith, in the "True Relation," supplies the name of the wounded sailor—Mathew Morton—which does not appear in the roster of the up-river expedition. On the basis of the

[4] Reprinted in L. G. Tyler, ed., *Narratives of Early Virginia* (volume V of *Original Narratives of Early American History*, ed. by J. F. Jameson. 19 vols., Charles Scribner's Sons, New York, 1906–1914), 5–23.

evidence derived from the three documents, then, the argument for the authorship of the anonymous "Relatyon" runs thus: Archer was wounded in the first encounter with the Indians in the Chesapeake region, the only other person wounded being a common sailor; Archer was a member of Newport's expedition, the sailor was not; the writer of the "Relatyon" showed wounds which could have been none other than Archer's; if these wounds were his own, the writer must have been Archer. Although not proved, the most plausible hypothesis is that Archer was the writer and showed his own wounds.

When the authorship of a document is attributable with certainty to some member of a small group all members of which are known, there is a well-defined method of determining which of them is the author. It consists of a comparison of the tricks of style displayed by the document in question with those found in the indubitable writings of each member of the group in turn. A case in point is the question of the authorship of certain numbers of *The Federalist*, the famous essays by Madison, Hamilton, and Jay advocating the ratification of the Federal Constitution.[5] Similarly, if the author of an anonymous writing can be plausibly conjectured, a comparison of the tricks of style found in the document with those shown by other writings known to be those of the conjectural author will reveal either a convincing similarity or a dissimilarity which will send the critic in pursuit of other clues. On such grounds John Smith could be dismissed as the possible author of the "Relatyon."

Not infrequently a problem of authorship arises in the case of documents ascribed to public men who employ advisers or other assistants in the preparation of their papers. President Washington consulted James Madison when he began to plan his Farewell Address, and Madison drafted a portion of it, embodying the President's suggestions. Later, at Washington's request, Alexander Hamilton extended and completed the draft,

---

[5] See the essay by Edward Gaylord Bourne, on "The Authorship of the Federalist," in his *Essays in Historical Criticism.* Charles Scribner's Sons, New York, 1901.

incorporating other suggestions of Washington's. For the critical historian the question emerges, which of the three men was the real author of the Address, or what was the share of each in producing it? By the method described, it may be concluded that the language is not that of Washington. In that case, the deeper problem remains, whether the Address embodies Washington's ideas and views expressed in the language of another.

A similar problem is connected with the presidential messages of Andrew Johnson. There is good reason for attributing some of them to George Bancroft, so far as the literary form is concerned. Whether they faithfully reflect Johnson's views is of much more fundamental importance.[6] If the putative author is the responsible source of the ideas set forth, he is the real author, even if the literary form is that of another.

Almost at the other extreme is the product of the "ghost writer," who supplies the facts and ideas as well as the form, leaving the putative author nothing to do save to sign his name, pay the "ghost," and enjoy his unearned reputation. Still a different problem is created by the plagiarist, who borrows both words and ideas of others without using quotation marks or giving credit. This form of spurious document will be discussed presently. Problems of authorship present all degrees of complexity.

A different phase of criticism relates to the *time* of the production of the document. Ordinarily publication dates, copyright dates, or other definite indications leave no uncertainty on this point, but sometimes it is necessary to seek other evidence. Suppose that a fragment of an old atlas comes to hand, minus title page and all indications of date of publication save those afforded by the maps themselves. One of these shows Texas as a state of Mexico, proving that publication of the atlas preceded 1836. Another shows Missouri as a State, fixing the

[6] William A. Dunning, "More Light on Andrew Johnson." *American Historical Review*, XI, 574–594 (April, 1906). *Cf.* communication of Carl Russell Fish on same subject, *ibid.*, XI, 951–952 (July, 1906), and article by Dunning in Massachusetts Historical Society *Proceedings*, 2 ser., XIX (Boston, 1906).

date of publication (if one possesses some knowledge of historical geography) as later than 1821. Careful scrutiny, aided by a knowledge of local history, narrows the gap between these dates still more, for the maps show the towns of Ann Arbor, Mich., and Fayette, Mo., both of which were founded about the mid-twenties. By continuing this process the date limits within which publication must have occurred might be brought almost together.

In the case of documents, the language used, the events alluded to, and even the spirit or temper, may be made to betray the time of origin, if the critic is adequately equipped for interpreting the clues he finds.

iii. DETECTION OF SPURIOUS DOCUMENTS

The means employed in determining authorship and time of origin are often effective also in detecting spurious documents. Forgers naturally attempt to disguise their deception by counterfeiting the language and temper of the times and persons represented, but they are quite likely to betray themselves by anachronisms or errors of other kinds. One of the most famous forgeries ever exposed by external criticism was that known as the "False Decretals." As early as the ninth century the papal archives contained certain alleged decrees of early popes, as well as a document purporting to be a donation, by the Emperor Constantine to Pope Sylvester, of the right to govern Italy and the rest of the Roman Empire in the West. Both decretals and donation were accepted as genuine during the Middle Ages, but modern critics have proved their falsity.

Their form does not correspond to the official form of such documents in the particular papal reigns to which the compiler assigned them. This diplomatics has shown. They use a method of dating which chronology has proved to be unhistorical. Although they supposedly belong to different centuries, their Latin style remains the same, and this the Frankish Latin of the ninth century. Philology has contributed this. It has also been found that their quotations from the scriptures were from the version of Jerome, amended during the time of Charlemagne, and that they contain passages taken bodily from a Frankish council of 829. Finally, they imply the view that the theology of the ninth century was the theology of the second, and that the early bishops of Rome exercised the same wide jurisdiction as the ninth-century popes. . . . It is probable that the collection originated in the diocese of Rheims between 847 and 865. . . .[7]

That American historians have need to be on guard against spurious documents could be shown by many illustrations. Hardly two years have elapsed since one of the leading monthly magazines suspended publication of a series of alleged letters of Abraham Lincoln, because their genuineness was found to be open to serious question. Errors of which Lincoln could hardly have been guilty figure prominently in the case against them. Thus in one, dated May 9, 1834, he is made to allude to "that North East quarter of Section 40." Since the system of land surveys established by Congress in 1785 provided for townships of thirty-six sections each, a "section 40" would have been unthinkable to Lincoln, who was himself an experienced surveyor.

Again in the same letter Lincoln is made to say that a family named Bixby is "leaving this week for Kansas." Since the territory of Kansas was not organized and opened for settlement until 1854, the passage seems clearly to be an anachronism, especially as it is very doubtful whether even the name "Kansas" was ever used for the region as early as 1834.[8]

Plagiarisms are detected readily enough when the work containing them is compared with that from which they are taken. However, if the original is obscure the plagiarism may escape notice for a long time. As in the case of anonymous documents,

[7] Henry E. Bourne, *The Teaching of History and Civics* (Longmans, Green and Company, New York, 1903), 35, n. 1. "Probably the authors believed that by representing the priesthood as an institution going back to the very beginnings of the church, they were doing the very best thing they could to make it effective in its holy work."—Ephraim Emerton, *Mediæval Europe 814–1300* (Ginn & Company, Boston, 1895), 79.

[8] For a shrewd critique of these letters, employing many principles of criticism, see Paul M. Angle, "The Minor Collection: A Criticism," in *Atlantic Monthly*, CXLIII, 516–525 (April, 1929).

the discovery of the facts is most likely to come from some one thoroughly conversant with all of the documents in the class to which the plagiarized one belongs, although sometimes the detection comes about through pure accident. Dr. Reuben G. Thwaites included in the series of reprints known as *Early Western Travels* one which was later shown by Dr. Milo M. Quaife to be in large part plagiarized.[9]

It makes little difference to the historian whether a spurious document originated in fraud or error. An example of one which obtained wide currency through an error is found in the instrument which was for a long time generally supposed to be the plan for the Federal Constitution which Charles Pinckney of South Carolina offered in the Convention of 1787. The story runs thus:

In 1819 John Quincy Adams, Secretary of State, in accordance with a resolution of Congress, prepared for publication the records of the Convention which had reposed in the files of the State Department since 1796. In the manuscript of the official journal he found a minute showing that Pinckney had submitted a plan, but there was no copy of it among the papers. Thereupon he wrote to Pinckney requesting him to supply a copy of the missing document. In reply Pinckney transmitted a paper which he said he thought was a copy of the plan he had submitted. However, he found among his papers "several rough drafts of the Constitution I proposed to the Convention," and he was uncertain which was the exact form submitted.

Without further effort to check the accuracy of Pinckney's selection, the Secretary of State inserted the paper in the proper place in the *Journal*, which was the title of the volume which he gave to the public. The document which he thus labeled the Pinckney Plan proved to be spurious.

James Madison, who had taken very full notes of the discussions in Convention, noticed, as soon as the *Journal* came to his attention, that the alleged Pinckney Plan did not harmonize with the evidence in his possession. In contemporary

[9] "Critical Evaluation of the Sources for Western History," *Mississippi Valley Historical Review*, I, 167–184 (Sept., 1914).

letters he declared that the published document could not possibly be the plan which Pinckney had submitted. The public, however, heard little or nothing of his doubts; and there was irony in the fact that when his own papers were published, a few years after his death, the editor borrowed the spurious Pinckney Plan from the *Journal* and gave it new currency by inserting it in Madison's notes on the debates of the Convention.

In this way uncritical writers were led to use the spurious document. Its marked similarity to the Constitution as adopted led many persons to hail Pinckney as the real father of our instrument of government, notwithstanding that the record of the Convention's proceedings showed conclusively that the basis of discussion was the Randolph Resolutions, and that Pinckney's Plan was referred to the Committee of Detail and not at any time considered in the Convention. Special students of the Constitution more shrewdly conjectured that the original form of the Pinckney Plan was lost, and that the alleged Plan was a copy of one of the preliminary drafts of the Constitution prepared by the Committee of Detail.[10] This conjecture proved to be correct.

At about the time this conjecture was formed, fresh interest was aroused in the probable character of the real Pinckney Plan, and the critics set themselves to examine all available evidence as to its provisions. The procedure was a very interesting example of constructive criticism, involving the careful comparison of all the existing documents containing hints of Pinckney's views on the Constitution, especially his own utterances before, in, and after the Convention. The findings thus reached were dramatically confirmed by the discovery of a fragmentary copy of the lost original.[11]

One result is that the original proposals of Pinckney are now

----

[10] Max Farrand, *The Records of the Federal Convention*, III, Appendix D, 595–609, and references in footnotes. Hereafter, this work will be cited as Farrand, *Records*. The work done on the problem of the Pinckney Plan is a brilliant piece of recent criticism which may be studied to excellent advantage by beginners.

[11] *Ibid.*

known in essence. Another is that when one encounters references to the provisions of the Pinckney Plan (which are by no means infrequent in articles in periodicals touching constitutional questions), one must know whether the writer has used the spurious document or the restored one. Unfortunately, knowledge of the latter is still confined almost wholly to a small group of specialists, and citations of the unauthentic instrument vitiate much otherwise intelligent writing. No constitutional discussion prior to the present century, if it turns upon provisions of the Pinckney Plan, can be trusted. There could not well be a more pointed illustration of the evil consequences of using documents not known to be authentic.

b. *Question of Original Form of Document: Textual Criticism*

The foregoing description of the methods of detecting spurious documents might logically have been introduced as a phase of the question of original form. However, even a genuine document may contain text corruptions, which are essentially spurious elements, misleading to the historian unless they can be eliminated and the original reading restored. The process by which this is done is known as textual criticism, and is so intricate that in some fields of history it has given rise to experts who devote themselves almost exclusively to such tasks, each working in a field sufficiently restricted to permit a very wide acquaintance with the texts which must be used in making comparisons, as well as a complete mastery of the appropriate auxiliary sciences.[12]

Such specialists are not strictly historians, unless they write history as well as criticize documents. Their function is to provide the writer with authentic documents and pure readings, and this is, of course, an essential preliminary of sound historical composition, yet not a part of it even when performed by the

---

[12] Textual criticism is just as necessary in the case of literary texts as in those relating to history, and the procedure is essentially the same for both classes of documents. The efforts to reproduce the original forms of Biblical texts, the works of ancient Greek and Latin writers, and the plays of Shakespeare rest upon the same principles.

historian himself. Textual criticism is at most the handmaid of the historian, who should ever regard composition as his proper task. Yet, although great collections of carefully edited documents now exist in all civilized countries, the historian must on occasion criticize texts for himself, and must always be on guard lest he be misled by the use of impure texts.

i. ORIGIN OF CORRUPTIONS

Corruptions, by which is meant any kind of deviations from the original, creep into documents in many ways, but chiefly through careless copying by scribe, typist, or printer. Where the original is preserved, the only safe course for the writer is to compare the copy which he intends to use with this original— a process called collation. John Quincy Adams records in his diary that upon one occasion he was charged with publishing an incorrect version of the Constitution. The critic, however, had not compared the Adams version with the original manuscript, and when Adams inspected the original he found that both his version and that consulted by the critic were incorrect![13]

Many an error creeps into the work of the historian through failure to check documents by the original. One great advantage of photostat copies lies in the absolute elimination of copyists' errors. Where the copies used are written, typed, or even printed, collation should be resorted to wherever possible. This is not always practicable. One can seldom go behind the official printed forms in government publications, although even these, as the foregoing example shows, cannot be accepted unquestioningly as exact. It is always desirable to check them if possible.[14]

When documents are published, it is the common practice to print them in such a form that corruptions and interpolations become indistinguishable from the original text. If the historian

[13] *Memoirs* . . . ed. by Charles Francis Adams (12 vols., J. B. Lippincott & Co., Philadelphia, 1874–1877), VI, 124–127.
[14] This rule of collation holds throughout the process of composition and publication. Copy for the printer should be carefully collated, and printer's proof should likewise be compared with the original or collated copy.

has access to the original manuscript, his advantage over the user of the printed version is obvious. When the diary of Gideon Welles, a member of Johnson's cabinet, was first published (1911), it was rightly hailed as a valuable addition to the contemporary evidence bearing on various problems of that troubled administration. When, however, some time afterwards, a scholar examined the manuscript and called attention to the fact that interpolations had been incorporated in the published diary as if a part of the original entries, its value was distinctly lessened.[15]

A classical example of the way in which corruptions occur is afforded by the history of Madison's notes on the debates of the Constitutional Convention. When the *Journal*, edited by Adams, was published, more than thirty years after the Convention, Madison compared his notes with it and detected certain errors in it. At the same time he changed his notes in numerous places where it seemed to him that the *Journal* was correct and his notes wrong. In other words, he trusted his *memory*, after the lapse of a generation, as a safe judge between the two records where they differed, and unfortunately, as critics have been able to demonstrate, in nearly every instance he substituted an erroneous reading for his own originally correct record. By this and other attempts at revision, previous to his death in 1836, Madison succeeded in corrupting his notes to a lamentable extent. When they were published in 1840 all of these changes were embodied with the original text and printed in uniform type, without a suggestion that the whole was not in the original notes.[16]

This corrupt edition of Madison's notes was the chief source of knowledge of the proceedings in Convention during the remainder of the nineteenth century. Near its close the Government printed an edition reproducing, as well as could be done in type, the actual form of the manuscript, showing both

[15] Howard K. Beale, "Is the Printed Diary of Gideon Welles Reliable?" *Am. Hist. Rev.*, XXX, 547 *et seq.* (April, 1925).
[16] Henry D. Gilpin, ed., *The Papers of James Madison.* Washington, 1840.

the original text and all changes, and giving the historical fraternity at large for the first time a trustworthy reprint.[17]

American history has been of such brief duration that the loss of important originals, although too frequent, has been slight in comparison with the losses which Europe has sustained. The scholarship of the Old World has frequently confronted the necessity of attempting to recover from impure copies the reading of lost originals. Where extant copies differ it is impossible, of course, for all of them to be correct. It may be that none of the variant readings is like the original. Nor does identity of wording in copies prove that they have preserved the original reading; it means only that the identical passages reproduce the same early form, or archetype. If the archetype faithfully reproduced the original, the extant copies may do so also, but if it was corrupt, the identity of the derived copies means only that they have perpetuated the corruptions. The problem here centers around the archetype, which may be lost like the original, the question being, Did it accurately preserve the original, or did it contain corruptions?

ii. CONJECTURAL EMENDATION

When there are no variant readings, and the extant reading is questionable, the critic's only recourse is to the method of conjectural emendation. Minor corrections are sometimes easily made by this method, as in the case of words which are repeated through the inadvertence of the scribe. The meaningless repetition of such words as "and," "the," or "that" is clearly the result of careless copying.[18]

If a passage is meaningless a corruption is strongly suggested, and context often aids in supplying a plausible reading. A certain textbook quotes President Hayes as saying in a message to Congress that an isthmian canal "would be vitally a part of our coast line." Clearly the word "vitally" is a slip, and

---

[17] Department of State: Bureau of Rolls and Library, *Documentary History of the Constitution*, III.

[18] Of course it is not impossible for an original to contain such errors, in which case emendation would not restore its form, but would improve upon it.

"virtually" is intended. The similar appearance of the two words misled a careless compositor, and the proof reader failed to catch the error.

There is grave danger that emendations may introduce new corruptions, if resorted to where the correct reading is not perfectly obvious. Undoubtedly many Shakespearian critics have violated the great dramatist's texts by well meant efforts to correct passages which they assumed to be corrupt because the meaning was not clear to them. The wise critic will be cautious. In the instance cited, the accuracy of the quotation can be checked by referring to Hayes' message in the proper government publication. If this were impossible the safe procedure for the critic who wished to quote and correct this passage in the textbook would be to insert his conjectural reading in brackets, thus: "would be vitally [virtually] a part of our coast line."

A famous example of successful conjectural emendation is that which J. N. Madvig performed in the case of a passage in one of Seneca's letters. The extant reading at the point of difficulty ran thus:

> Philosophia unde dicta sit, apparet; ipso enim nomine fatetur.
> Quidam et sapientiam ita quidam finierunt, ut dicerent divinorum
> et humanorum sapientiam . . .

The profounder the critic's knowledge of classical Latin, the clearer it was that these words did not make sense, and that the reading must be corrupt. For a long time the conjecture of scholars was that words had been dropped between *ita* and *quidam*. Madvig, who supplemented his Latin with a knowledge of paleography, pictured to himself the passage as it must have appeared in the lost archetype, written in capitals, without spaces between words or sentences, and without any marks of punctuation, thus (in part):

> . . . NOMINEFATETURQUIDAMETSAPIENTIAM. . . .

It was then easy to surmise that some thoughtless copyist, whose manuscript had since been followed, had wrongly divided the words. Madvig's final step was to make sentence and word divisions at two new points, suggested by the context, thus at once bringing out the meaning. His emendation consisted solely in making these divisions:

> . . . nomine fatetur quid amet. Sapientiam. . . . [19]

iii. VARIANT READINGS

When dealing with variant readings, the critic's first step is to determine, so far as possible, the interrelationships of the copies in which the variations occur. If A is the lost original, B and C may be independent copies of it, and D may be a copy of B. Or D may be copied in part from A and in part from C, reproducing some of the latter's corruptions and introducing some of its own. An almost endless variety of interrelationships is possible; but whenever criticism reveals that one copy is derived from another, or others, that one is eliminated, and this process of elimination is continued until there remain only independent copies.

The divergent readings of these independent copies are then compared, and any available external evidence is brought to bear, in the effort to determine the correct reading. One must beware of accepting a reading merely because it occurs oftener than others. One document may have the original reading while a dozen which agree in another reading may be incorrect; or all may be incorrect. Certainty of conclusion is often almost impossible, and one must be content with what one finally adjudges, in the light of all the evidence, to be the most plausible reading.

An illustration from American history is found in the resolutions introduced at an early session of the Federal Convention of 1787 and made the basis of its discussions.[20] The original draft, presented by Edmund Randolph, long since disappeared. The

---

[19] Ch. V. Langlois and Ch. Seignobos, *Introduction to the Study of History*, 78–79.

[20] John Franklin Jameson, "Studies in the History of the Federal Convention" (American Historical Association *Annual Report* for 1902, I, 89–167), 103–111.

delegates, however, seem to have made copies for their individual use, and a few copies of these copies are still in existence. No two are alike, and there are reasons for thinking that none is without corruptions. The extant copies are in some cases at least three stages removed from the original: the delegates first copied the original more or less accurately; next they made changes in the course of debate; finally they recopied, embodying the changes in the papers which have been preserved. The desirability of restoring the original reading of the resolutions, if one is to study critically the Convention's progress, is evident.

For convenience the copies, in the form in which they have come down to us, may be designated as follows: One made by Madison will be called A. It is reproduced in the *Documentary History of the Constitution*.[21] Another, made by Brearly, will be called B. It is also to be found in the *Documentary History*.[22] A third, by Paterson, is in the New York Public Library and has never been printed. It will be called C. D designates the form found in the *Journal*, edited by Adams, and published in 1819. E denotes the form printed in Gilpin's edition of the Madison papers, published in 1840. F is the form found in Yates' *Secret Proceedings and Debates*, published in 1821. G is a form printed in the third edition of Elliot's *Debates*.

Critical comparison of these seven forms reveals their interrelationships and reduces the number of independent copies to three—A, B, and C. Copy D is found to be taken from B. Brearly's papers, including his copy of the resolutions, were deposited in the State Department by his executor. Adams used them in preparing the *Journal;* and there is no other source from which he could readily have obtained a copy of the resolutions. Slight discrepancies between D and B are attributable to his efforts to "restore" the original reading. E is professedly a copy of A, with an addition made by the editor on the warrant of a statement by Madison in a letter written in 1833. F is a copy of D. Yates records that he made a copy of the resolutions

[21] III, 17–20. [22] I, 332–335.

and preserved it with his notes, but when the latter were prepared for publication, the copy had disappeared, and the form
in the *Journal* was substituted. G reproduces B plus a "resolution 16." This resolution was in fact a motion made immediately
after the reading of the resolutions (as the *Journal* shows);
Elliot mistook it for one of the resolutions. D, E, F, and G are
thus all found to be copies derived directly or indirectly from
A or B, most of them with additional corruptions.

The variations in the wording of the three independent
copies, A, B, and C, occur in resolutions 4, 5, 6, 7, 9, 11, and 13.
Resolutions 1, 2, 3, 8, 10, 12, 14, and 15 agree, and are not under
suspicion, because, the copies *being independent*, the identity of
these portions could not be accounted for if the reading was
impure. If there were corruptions in these resolutions, identity
of reading would prove that the copies were not independent.
Identity of error proves interdependence.

Resolution 4, the first in which a variant reading occurs, is as
follows in A:

> Res^d that the members of the first branch of the National
> Legislature ought to be elected by the people of the several
> States every   [1]   for the term of   [2]   ; to be of the age of   [3]
> years at least, to receive liberal stipends by which they may be
> compensated for the devotion of their time to public service; to be
> ineligible to any office established by a particular State, or under
> the authority of the United States, except those peculiarly belong-
> ing to the functions of the first branch, during the term of service,
> and for the space of   [4]   after its expiration; to be incapable of
> reëlection for the space of   [5]   after the expiration of their term
> of service, and to be subject to recall.

B varies from A at the following points: (1) instead of the
second blank, the words "three years" occur; (2) instead of the
fourth blank, the words "one year" appear; (3) instead of the
fifth blank the words "one year" appear again.

C varies from B and agrees with A in having a blank space
where B reads "three years"; and varies from both A and B in
omitting entirely the words beginning with "to be incapable of"
and ending with "term of service."

't would be a plausible guess that the original resolution contained all of the blanks which appear in A, and that the words which appear at three of these points in B are due to interpolations by Brearly representing later decisions of the Convention. This conjecture is confirmed by external evidence. Fortunately the published records of the Convention are now quite full; not only is the official journal accessible in printed form, but also the notes of a number of the delegates.[23] These records are very useful in determining the original form of the resolutions. Madison's notes of the debate on June 12 show that the second and fourth blanks were filled on that day with the words found in B, and the notes of Yates and the record in the *Journal* confirm Madison. The *Journal*, in addition, shows that the last blank was filled, as in B, on that date.

This leaves the omission in C to be accounted for. It has been conjectured that Paterson simply overlooked these words when making his final copy.[24] A glance at the full resolution will show how easily he might have done so. The repetition of almost identical phraseology in adjacent lines, as here, is a common source of error on the part of copyists, since the eye is likely to light upon the phrase where it *recurs*, after it has been once copied, thus missing the intermediate words.

In the present instance there is another possibility, for the *Journal* of June 12 shows that the omitted clause was struck out on that day. If Paterson struck it out of his first copy in conformity with this action, the omission from his final copy, like the additions in Brearly's, was because he followed the changes made in the Convention. In either case the evidence indicates that the reading of A is correct.

Applying this method to resolutions 5, 6, 7, 11, and 13, in which variant readings occur, the critic arrives at the conclusion that A is correct. Madison doubtless made a more deliberate effort to preserve the original form in his copy, and avoided using it to record changes made in the course of discussion. Yet even Madison's copy comes under suspicion in the reading of the

[23] Farrand, *Records*, cited *supra*, n. 10.   [24] Jameson, *loc. cit.*, 111.

ninth resolution, and up to date all efforts of the critics have failed to give a reading for this resolution which can be certified as the original. The reading of A is as follows:

> Res.ᵈ that a National Judiciary be established to consist of one or more supreme tribunals, and of inferior tribunals to be chosen by the National Legislature, to hold their offices during good behaviour; and to receive punctually at stated times fixed compensation for their services, in which no increase or diminution shall be made so as to affect the persons actually in office at the time of such increase or diminution. that the jurisdiction of the inferior tribunals shall be to hear & determine in the first instance, and of the supreme tribunal to hear and determine in the dernier resort, all piracies & felonies on the high seas, captures from an enemy; cases in which foreigners or citizens of other States applying to such jurisdictions may be interested, or which respect the collection of the National revenue; impeachments of any National officers, and questions which may involve the national peace and harmony.

The reading of B agrees with that of A after the first sentence, but this sentence is quite different:

> That a National Judiciary be established to consist of one Supreme Tribunal, to hold their Offices during good behavior, and to receive punctually at stated times fixed compensation for their services. . . . etc.

C is like A except in having a blank before the words "inferior tribunals" in the first sentence.

None of these versions is satisfactory. A is questionable because it is not easy to think of more than one *supreme* tribunal, and because the phraseology at this point is inconsistent with that of the latter part of the resolution, where the jurisdiction of "*the* supreme tribunal" is defined.[25] B is likewise inconsistent, for the definition of the jurisdiction of the inferior tribunals, which it shares with A, requires a mention of them in the first sentence. C is open to the same criticism as A, although the blank before "inferior tribunals" suggests that the words "one or more" may have been later additions, intended to fill the blank, instead of going before "supreme tribunal."

[25] Italics author's.

The *Journal* for June 4 strengthens this conjecture, for on that day the resolution "that a National Judiciary be established" was adopted, after which the words were "added": "to consist of one supreme tribunal and of one or more inferior tribunals." Whether these words appeared now for the first time, or whether they were in the original resolution and were now "added" in the sense of being *also adopted*, is not clear. That the latter may have been the case appears from an entry in Paterson's notes for May 29, which indicates that the original resolution contained a clause providing for both supreme and inferior tribunals. Whether such a clause was in the original resolution or not, it is safe to conclude that the words "one or more" are misplaced in A and C.

As for B, on June 5, according to the *Journal*, Madison moved to strike out of the resolution the provision for "appointment by the Legislature." These words, then, must have been in the original, and Brearly must have struck them out because of this action.[26]

The jurisdiction clauses of the resolution present additional perplexities, but enough has been said to illustrate the procedure involved in attempts to restore original readings.

2. INTERNAL CRITICISM

When it has been decided that a document is genuine, when all that is possible has been done to make sure that its reading is true to the original, and when everything that can be learned about the time, place, and other circumstances connected with its origin is at the disposal of the critic, he is ready for the work of internal criticism.

The inquiry now shifts from *document* to *statement*, and it becomes the investigator's duty to make sure that he understands each statement which he intends to use. This phase of criticism is known as

---

[26] The *Journal* shows further that the words "and of one or more inferior tribunals" were struck out on June 5, thus giving further evidence that the words "one or more" accompanied the reference to the inferior tribunals instead of the supreme tribunal, and accounting also for a part of Brearly's omission.

a. *Positive Criticism*

It is particularly necessary to avoid reading into a statement a meaning which the maker did not intend to convey. There is a great temptation to make this mistake when one *wishes* or *hopes* to find a particular meaning in the statement, and the utmost care is required to avoid this form of intellectual dishonesty. The partisan is prone to misrepresent his opponents in this manner, and even the impartial historian who maintains an attitude of detached indifference towards partisan controversies is in danger of becoming so enamored with his theories or hypotheses that he will find support for them by twisting the meaning of statements. The quest must be for *truth*, even if it upsets one's pet hypotheses.

i. LITERAL MEANING OF STATEMENTS

The first question to be asked is, What does the statement say? The question may seem foolish, until one reflects that statements are often couched in a foreign language, or involve the use of unfamiliar terms, or familiar words in unwonted senses. Technical terms, obsolete words, references to customs or institutions which existed at remote times or in distant places, even when in one's own language, may convey as little meaning to the mind of the novice as if they were in an unknown tongue. Hence the difficulties of the young student who tries to read the plays of Shakespeare. When the immature person is set to study the first charter of Virginia, and reads therein that the lands granted to the Company are "To be holden of Us, our Heirs, and Successors, as of our Manor at *East-Greenwich* in the County of Kent, in free and common Soccage only, and not in Capite," the teacher should not be surprised to learn that the passage is "Greek" to him. The King James version of the Bible records that "Jacob sodd pottage," a statement which means little or nothing to one who does not know the modern equivalents of the words "sodd" and "pottage."

Even dissimilarities of spelling from period to period are disconcerting; such a passage as that quoted from Percy's "Discourse," on page 62, may prove to be difficult reading for twentieth-century students. The native name for one of the Indian villages near Jamestown, variously rendered by the first English settlers as "Kiskyack," and "Cheesecake," led one of the author's acquaintances to surmise that there were *Czechs* among the early immigrants to Virginia! Plainly the historian must have a wide knowledge of the language, laws, customs, and institutions of the country and period in which his labor lies, or he cannot even understand the documents with which he must work.

ii. REAL MEANING OF STATEMENTS

Having determined what a statement literally says, the critic must, if possible, ascertain whether it means what it says, for there is often a difference between the literal and real meanings. The critic is not here concerned primarily with the truthfulness of the statement. Rather he is concerned with discovering whether the statement is *intended* to be taken literally or in an oblique sense. To mistake an ironical saying, for instance, for the expression of the maker's real opinion is to take the literal meaning of words and miss the intent.

Yet such mistakes are frequent, and not easy to avoid. It is nearly always difficult to determine exactly what meaning figurative language is intended to convey, and often, indeed, not even easy to recognize a figure of speech. Preceding the House election of 1825, John Quincy Adams, as his diary records, received a letter from an anonymous correspondent, a partisan of a rival candidate, threatening to "raise the standard of revolt and civil war" if his favorite was defeated. These words might be taken literally or merely as a threat of persistent political opposition such as, in fact, followed Adams' election.

The historian is not infallible, but if he is fortunately possessed of sobriety of judgment, he will be saved from many a misinterpretation. Too often writers display the literal-mindedness of the student who wrote in a test paper, that in a certain campaign the Whigs did not frame a platform until the night before the election. The surprised teacher, upon investigation, found that the basis of this assertion was a statement in the textbook to the effect that the Whigs framed no platform until the *eve of the election!*

This phase of criticism is called "positive" because it is possible, sometimes at least, to obtain affirmative results. That is, it is possible to determine exactly what statements say and mean. In this character it stands in contrast with the results obtained by

b. *Negative Criticism*

It is because this phase of the critical process cannot determine the truth of statements that it is called "negative criticism." Indeed, its purpose is to discover every possible reason for *disbelieving.* It is the rule that every statement must be doubted so long as any reasonable ground for doubt can be found.

When external criticism has supplied data concerning the author of a statement and the circumstances under which it was made, the critic is in position to test it in many ways. It may be untrustworthy either because of some form of incompetence on the part of the author which prevents him from knowing the facts, or because of some form of untruthfulness which prevents him from telling the truth even when he knows it.

i. TESTS OF COMPETENCE

The first concern of the critic is to ascertain what opportunity the author of a statement had to know the facts. If he was an eye-witness, the presumption is, other things being equal, that he has given a more accurate account of what occurred than that which a person not present could give. But eye-witnesses are not equally good observers, and the critic must learn to discriminate among them. It must be remembered that in history as in science truth is established only upon the foundation of *reliable* observation. Any statement which deserves the serious attention of the historian must be found to rest ultimately upon such observation.

In recent years experimental psychology has contributed to the critical apparatus of historians by revealing how the human mind acts in certain situations. Perhaps the chief result has been an enhanced sense of the difference between competent and incompetent eye-witnesses, and a new emphasis upon the importance of *trained* observation. "If a witness should testify in court that he had seen a red cap at dusk but not a blue coat, his testimony would be discounted at once," for it has been established by experimental psychology that in a dim light blue is more visible than red.[27] "The tendency of the mind to fill in the gaps of sense impressions is a highly significant fact for the historian." [28]

Some years ago a bomb exploded in Wall Street, in New York City. Eight eye-witnesses testified that at the time there were a number of vehicles within a block of the spot, and that the bomb was carried upon a red motor truck. Another eye-witness testified that the bomb was in a horse-drawn truck, and that only one other vehicle was in sight. It was eventually proved that the eight witnesses were wrong and the one right. The advantage enjoyed by the one was due to the excited state of mind of the eight, which led them to confuse what they had actually seen with what had come into their minds afterwards. The ninth witness was an army officer whose experience had taught him to keep his wits under fire.[29]

Unusual emotional stress of any kind is likely to render observers incompetent. So, of course, does ignorance. The critic must determine whether any influences of these kinds operated upon the eye-witnesses. The rustic who prayed that the Lord would give him a visible sign that his sins were forgiven, by causing one of the stars to move, and who then believed that he actually saw a star move, may have experienced spiritual satisfaction, but is disqualified as a witness on astronomy.

Sometimes persons ranked as eye-witnesses were in **very**

[27] Johnson, *op. cit.*, 33, citing Hans Gross, *Criminal Psychology*, 206.
[28] Johnson, 31. See discussion *ibid.*, 25 *et seq.*
[29] *Ibid.*, 24, 25.

unfavorable positions for observing what went on, even when actually present. Theoretically the peace negotiations at Versailles at the close of the World War were conducted openly, in the presence of representatives of the press. Actually the room was so crowded that reporters generally stood in the adjacent halls, almost out of sight and sound of the speakers. A knowledge of this fact has an important bearing upon the historian's attitude towards their accounts of what was said and done.

An unfavorable position for observation may be due to the sheer negligence of a potentially competent observer. Edward W. Bok recounts in his autobiography how once while a youthful reporter on a New York daily, he was sent to "cover" a play. Having already seen it once, he felt certain that he could make a write-up *in absentia*, and yielded to the temptation to keep another appointment. In due time he turned in his "copy" but learned when too late that the performance had not been given, owing to the illness of the leading lady! [30]

More perfect conditions seldom exist for accurate reporting than those under which James Madison took his notes on the debates in the Federal Convention of 1787. He describes these conditions himself:

> In pursuance of the task I had assumed I chose a seat in front of the presiding member with the other members, on my right & left hands. In this favorable position for hearing all that passed, I noted in terms legible & in abbreviations & marks intelligible to myself what was read from the Chair or spoken by the members; and losing not a moment unnecessarily between the adjournment & reassembling of the Convention I was enabled to write out my daily notes during the session or within a few finishing days after its close in the extent and form preserved in my own hand on my files.
>
> In the labor and correctness of this I was not a little aided by practice, and by a familiarity with the style and train of observation and reasoning which characterized the principal speakers. It happened also that I was not absent a single day, nor more than a casual fraction of an hour in any day, so that I could not have lost a single speech, unless a very short one. . . .

[30] *The Americanization of Edward Bok* (8th edn., Charles Scribner's Sons, New York, 1921), 61–62.

> With a very few exceptions, the speeches were neither furnished, nor revised, nor sanctioned, by the speakers, but written out from my notes, aided by the freshness of my recollections.[31]

Here we have an intelligent, dispassionate, educated, painstaking, and experienced man, favorably placed for seeing and hearing. Careful comparison of his report with the fragmentary notes of other delegates reveals few important omissions or errors, except those due to his unfortunate efforts at revision many years after the original notes were taken.

Madison as a reporter contrasts significantly with Major William Jackson, employed by the Convention as its official secretary. The latter seems to have owed his appointment to influence rather than fitness.[32] Adams found that his minutes were hardly more than the notes from which full minutes should have been, but were not, written up.[33] Jackson, whom Adams consulted in 1819 when preparing the papers of the Convention for publication, had no recollections which could aid Adams in rescuing them from their "disorderly state," although he told Adams that he had taken extensive minutes with a view to publication.[34] When Jackson delivered the records of proceedings to Washington, as directed by the Convention, he first burned all the loose scraps of paper in his possession.[35] Among these quite possibly may have been copies of the Pinckney Plan and the Randolph resolutions, neither of which was copied into his minutes nor otherwise preserved by him. Such facts are significant to the historian who wishes to judge between Jackson and Madison as "eye-witnesses" and reporters of the Convention's doings.

The testimony of eye-witnesses, however subject to suspicion it may seem to be, must be made the starting point of investigation. But an absentee who has been trained to reason accurately from complex and imperfect data may be able to make a statement by way of conclusion that is far more reliable than that of

[31] Farrand, *Records*, III, 550.
[32] *Ibid.*, I, xii, note 6.
[33] *Ibid.*, III, 433.
[34] *Ibid.*, 426.
[35] *Ibid.*, 82.

the ordinary eye-witness. This possibility is what justifies trials in court, inquests, and official investigations of all kinds; and it affords the only ground for believing that the trained historian can tell a more truthful tale than the sources.

At its best, the work of writers for the public press approximates that of the critical historian. Special correspondents are often highly trained men who take great pains to make statements which may be relied upon. For the most part, however, it is unfair to hold newspaper reporters to the same standards of accuracy which are required of the historian. Bok's negligence, to be sure, was extreme, and almost cost him his position; yet the conditions under which a reporter ordinarily works excuse him from any prolonged effort to sift evidence and ascertain facts in detail. In the few minutes which he can spend upon the spot where a "news event" has occurred, especially if it is of an unforeseen kind, and has taken place before his arrival, he cannot do much more than interview such persons as may be within reach. They may or may not have been eye-witnesses; they may or may not be intelligent. What he hears he sends in, interlarded with such phrases as "it is said," and "it is alleged." Thus he neither assumes responsibility for the truth of assertions nor fixes it upon anyone else. If the accident or other event which he reports actually occurred, he is not held to a very strict accountability for details, such as, who was at fault or what the damage amounted to in dollars.

Something more may be expected where the reporter has covered a public meeting, such as a political convention, and was therefore an eye- and ear-witness; but the accuracy of statements will vary with the personal qualities of the individual reporter and the conditions under which he does his work. Standards are none too exacting. Reports of interviews with prominent personages are notoriously inaccurate. It would seem that the newspaper man is often indifferent as to whether he repeats the exact words of an interview, and for this reason many persons refuse to grant them, or permit them only upon condition that copy be submitted for approval before publication.

Reports of public speeches likewise often attribute to the speakers utterances very different from those actually made.

For all these reasons the historian who uses newspapers as sources (and they are of very great value) must take pains to check all statements with great care. It must be remembered, too, that newspapers include matter of many different kinds, and the critic's attitude must vary with the class of items dealt with. Advertisements often have their uses for him, and obviously differ from editorials from the point of view of the type of criticism to be applied. Weekly and monthly news journals, moreover, are more trustworthy than the dailies, since the articles in them are prepared more carefully and deliberately. In sum, statements in newspapers are subject to the tests applicable to statements of other kinds, with rather more than the usual amount of suspicion that they may have been made by rather negligent persons.[36]

Great masses of source material of a kind with which the historian has much to do are found in diaries, memoirs, recollections, and autobiographies. The trustworthiness of these differs greatly. The writers are not equally truthful and competent, and if they were, the appraisal of their statements would still differ. A contemporary record, such as is made in a diary, is more likely to be accurate than a memoir written long after the events recounted. For this reason the critic is more inclined to believe John Quincy Adams's assertion in 1844 that Andrew Jackson approved, a quarter of a century earlier, the relinquishment of the claim of the United States to Texas, than to accept Jackson's denial, for the former made an entry to this effect in his notable diary, at the time, while in 1844 Jackson spoke from memory only.

Old people's recollections are notoriously fallible. In 1925 a graduate student in The Ohio State University personally interviewed an aged politician concerning his attitude towards Mr. Bryan during the campaign of 1896, and was informed by

---

[36] *Cf.* James Ford Rhodes, "Newspapers as Historical Sources," in *Historical Essays*, 81-97; Spahr and Swenson, *op cit*, 120-121, and note 6.

the gentleman that he had been unable to follow Mr. Bryan's leadership. Later the student found contemporary accounts of speeches by this Ohio politician, advocating Mr. Bryan's election.

During the gold rush of 1849 a young Philadelphian went to California, where he remained for five or six years. Thirty-five years later he wrote from memory an account of his wanderings and adventures. In this he says: "While the Events recorded are yet bright in my mind and strictly true and correct, it is possible that some of them may be placed out of time and out of the exact location." [37] In fact the critic is compelled to doubt the accuracy of details of all kinds in a book of this type, although the composite picture afforded by many such works may be trustworthy in a broad impressionistic way. [38]

While a contemporary record, such as a diary, escapes the danger to which memoirs are exposed through lapses of memory, it cannot be any more accurate and dependable than its author. The personal equation enters here, as in all statements. An incompetent eye-witness will make an imperfect report, whether it be in a court of law or in a private diary. An untrained person may mistake hearsay for fact. A prejudiced mind will be reflected in comments on men and events. John Quincy Adams, while an accurate recorder of events, was prone to include in his diary his own interpretations of the actions of others, based often on the assumption of unworthy motives on their part.

The rule that in order to get at the truth statements must be traced to their basis in reliable observation means, in one application, that the critic must inquire whether a statement under scrutiny is based on the observation of the maker or on that of others. It has already been recognized that while the conclusions of a careful investigator belong in the second category, they may be so sound as to be considered authoritative. However, if the critic is not satisfied that this is the case, or if he is working upon an original and unsolved problem, he must

[37] Anna Paschall Hannum, ed., *A Quaker Forty-Niner: The Adventures of Charles Edward Pancoast on the American Frontier* (University of Pennsylvania Press, Philadelphia, 1930), 392.

[38] See discussion on page 98 *et seq.*

not be content with second- and third-hand assertions or opinions, if it is possible to go behind them to the first-hand accounts.
Hence the emphasis that is placed upon the sources.

Nothing is more common than for persons to repeat, often
with embellishments, what others have told them, without any
attempt to ascertain the truth. So rumor spreads and slander
grows. Henry Ward Beecher once wrote a letter to a Congress-
man in which he said that Postmaster Lincoln of Brooklyn had
told him that Senator Pomeroy of Kansas had told him that he
had called at the White House and found "the President
[Johnson], his son, and son-in-law, all drunk and unfit for
business, and that the President kept a mistress at the White
House." The member of Congress sent Beecher's letter to
Secretary Hugh McCulloch, who showed it to Secretary Gideon
Welles, of the Navy Department. When as a result Johnson's
friends demanded an explanation from Pomeroy, he disavowed
making any of the charges except that he had seen Robert
Johnson "in liquor," and had thought that the son-in-law was
in the same condition.[39]

A historian who encountered Beecher's letter and, confiding
in his excellent reputation, used it as evidence bearing on
Johnson's character without tracing the charges to their source,
would obviously be led to a false conclusion. True criticism is
intolerant of such slovenly procedure. Yet histories of the
United States abound in stories which have originated in malice
and error, have been disseminated by partisan propagandists,
accepted by uncritical historians, and copied and perpetuated
by their successors. To restate the point here made, a person
who merely passes along what he has heard is an incompetent
witness, whom the critic should thrust aside in his quest for the
responsible author of the assertion.

Even the most careful historian will sometimes be deceived
by supposing that he has ferreted out the ultimate facts when
there is additional evidence of which he has not become aware.

[39] Howard K. Beale, *The Critical Year* (Harcourt, Brace and Company, New
York [c 1930]), 78–79.

The unknown facts may even lead to a directly opposite conclusion. The two quotations which follow tell their own story and teach their own lesson:

> Many of the most wealthy and influential houses in colonial Virginia were founded by men that could boast of no social prominence in England. . . . Adam Thoroughgood, although he came to Virginia as a servant or apprentice, became wealthy and powerful.[40]

> The different records . . . show the continued emigration to Virginia of numerous persons who were connected by ties of blood or marriage with persons of high position in England. . . . Adam Thoroughgood . . . was a brother of Sir John Thoroughgood . . . who was attached to the Court.[41]

A word or two must be said about legends and traditions. The truth is that the historian can make nothing of them of any positive value, in the absence of corroboratory evidence of a documentary, archæological, or other kind, for the simple reason that they cannot be traced to their origins. And without a knowledge of origins the ordinary critical tests cannot be applied.

ii. TESTS OF TRUTHFULNESS

The statement of a person who, for any of the reasons which have been considered, is an incompetent witness, must be regarded as doubtful. It does not follow, on the other hand, that all statements of potentially competent witnesses are true. The question of whether a competent witness is also truthful is, indeed, quite a distinct one. He may know the facts and yet fail to tell them truthfully. This may be because he falsifies deliberately and intentionally; but the problem is not merely one of veracity. Influences of various kinds may lead to the distortion or coloring of a statement so that it misses the truth in one way or other without a deliberate falsification.

It is always wise to inquire whether the maker of a statement

[40] Thomas J. Wertenbaker, *Patrician and Plebeian in Virginia* (published by the author, Charlottesville, Va., 1910), 17.

[41] Philip Alexander Bruce, *Social Life in Virginia in the Seventeenth Century* (printed for the author by Whittet and Shepperson, Richmond, 1907), 51–52.

had a personal interest of any kind to be promoted by having his statement believed. One can hardly expect anything but denial from a person accused of crime, nor anything but fair promises from a candidate for office. Most people have learned to take the representations of sales solicitors with a grain of salt. A subordinate is expected to speak well of his superiors, at least in public, and when a discharged employee denounces the conduct or policies of his former employer, he is to be suspected of pique or a desire for vengeance. The critic should learn the present and past relationships between persons who make statements and those about whom they are made. Those who accept assertions by interested parties without further ado are childishly credulous or the victims of their own desire to believe regardless of the evidence.

To what race, nation, party, sect, social set, profession, or other group did the maker of the statement belong? It is important to answer this question because a prejudice favorable to such group is to be apprehended, which would tend to warp assertions from the exact truth. The critic must be constantly on the outlook for the effects of prejudice, for no one is ever entirely free from it. He must, for example, approach the work of Catholic and Protestant historians of the Reformation prepared in both cases to find the subject treated with more or less of bias in spite of the utmost efforts of the authors to be fair and impartial. Nor could he expect the same point of view from two historians of labor struggles, if one had a capitalistic background and the other socialistic proclivities.

George Bancroft's account of the Battle of Lexington shows a national bias which does violence to the facts. Depositions signed by many Americans who took part in the battle, including Captain Parker who was in command, show that Parker gave the order to disperse upon the approach of the British, before the British officer, Pitcairn, commanded it. Bancroft had copies of these depositions, yet his story of the combat is a pæan of praise for men who "stood motionless in the ranks, witnesses against aggression; too few to resist, too brave to fly." According to Bancroft (but not the sources), Pitcairn, seeing that the Americans heeded not his command, "discharged a pistol, and with a loud voice cried, 'Fire!'" and then, "in the disparity of numbers, Parker ordered his men to disperse. Then, and not till then, did a few of them, on their own impulse, return the British fire." [42] As a matter of fact, it is impossible, in the light of the available evidence, to determine which side fired the first shot. Bancroft is content to state a conclusion shaped by his own patriotic desires.

Since it is to be expected that interest or prejudice will result in statements in which the truth is more or less colored, statements which might be expected to show such prejudice but do not are apparently placed on a somewhat higher level of credibility. Especially is this true when the slant is *unfavorable* to the personal or group interest of the author. The Bible commends the man who "sweareth to his own hurt and changeth not." Nevertheless the critic must be on guard against covert motives. A longing for notoriety has caused many a crime, and the same motive or others arising from perverted mentality has led many a person to confess a crime which he did not commit. A clever liar, moreover, may seek to throw the critic off guard by a false show of fairness, in order to gain acceptance of statements detrimental to opponents, and really favorable to himself. If an incoming official speaks in complimentary terms of his retiring predecessor of the opposite party, it may mean only that he wishes to be thought magnanimous. It is therefore worth while to repeat that each statement must be tested separately, and also in the light of all related statements.

It is often wise for a writer to volunteer information about his relations with his subject, in order to disarm suspicion of bias. In his recent history of the Adams family (the family of John Adams) James Truslow Adams promptly disavows kinship with his subjects, since kinship would create a presumption of

---

[42] George Bancroft, *History of the United States of America, from the Discovery of the Continent* (author's last revision: 6 vols., D. Appleton and Company, New York, 1891–1892), IV, 155.

friendly bias. Such a presumption is always in order where people make statements concerning their kindred, although critical examination may prove the presumption to be unwarranted. Nor is the bias in cases where it exists by any means always friendly; often it is quite the reverse.

A protestation of impartiality should arouse suspicion. A favorable comment is often the prelude to an unfavorable remark, and should be considered as an inseparable part of it. On the other hand, an expression of admiration for members of an opposed or contrasted group, if not followed by any comment of a different tone, is evidence of absence of the customary bias. If an account of Catholic missions among the western Indians, written by a Protestant, is uniformly sympathetic and appreciative, the impression of impartiality is strengthened by a statement making clear the writer's own religious affiliations. Any conclusions based on such statements, however, should be tentative, and should stand or fall only after examination of all related statements.

A third type of inquiry asks whether the position of the maker of a statement was such as to require or permit conventional expressions rather than the utterance of his own true sentiments. The pious phrases of the President of the United States in the annual proclamation of a Day of Thanksgiving are worth nothing as evidence of his personal views on religion; nor does the signature "Yours truly" warrant a young woman in bringing a breach of promise suit against her masculine correspondent. In days gone by men wrote letters to their deadliest enemies and signed themselves "Your obedient servant." The meaninglessness of formulæ is plain enough in such cases as the last two, but some persons might not readily perceive that the same is equally true in the first. The danger of misconstruction increases in direct ratio with the critic's unfamiliarity with the class of documents in which the formulæ are found, because of the greater difficulty in recognizing them.

Somewhat similar are expressions uttered under such circumstances that they were likely to be colored by the desire to please hearers or readers. The courtier's words in addressing the king are not the only instances of studied flattery. It is often thought better to be complacent and agreeable than to utter unpleasant truths. Courtesy sometimes demands silence or words which do not reveal the speaker's whole thought. The honest efforts of young orators and debaters, however crude, elicit praise more often than frank and constructive but chilling criticism. A recommendation addressed To Whom It May Concern, and handed to the person recommended, is likely to be less candid and consequently to carry less weight than if addressed confidentially to a prospective employer. Sheer laziness and desire to avoid irritating discussion ofttimes induces people to acquiesce in opinions which they do not share. Thousands of persons sign petitions to be rid of the bearers, whether the petitions express their desires or not.

Internal evidence often suggests pertinent criticisms. If a writer betrays vanity, by the habitual ascription to himself of a conspicuous share in important actions or events, intimacy with prominent personages, or otherwise, doubts of his truthfulness are aroused. Such bragging ways supply the chief reasons for questioning John Smith's story of his rescue by Pocahontas. A boastful tone pervades all of Smith's writings; yet in his first account of his capture by the Indians there is not a word suggestive of intervention by the native princess at a moment of peril. It was not until her marriage with John Rolfe, followed by her spectacular reception in England, had made her a celebrity (and, say the critics, not until her death had made denial of the account impossible), that Smith published the story of the rescue.

If internal evidence betrays a strong interest in literary form or effects on the part of a writer, there is reason to fear that the facts are distorted. Although a pleasing style is worth striving for, historical accuracy is almost certain to suffer if a writer's chief motive becomes literary.[43] The love of rhetorical flour-

---

[43] Homer C. Hockett, "The Literary Motive in the Writing of History," *Miss. Val. Hist. Rev.*, XII, 469–482 (March, 1926).

ishes, picturesque detail, dramatic narrative, or a fondness for portraying intense emotion or conduct of extraordinary nobility, may supplant the desire to tell the precise truth. An example of the last kind is the Parson Weems story of George Washington and the cherry tree. Bancroft wrote in almost as exaggerated a strain when he described the actions and feelings of the people of Lexington upon the news of the approach of the British troops on the morning of April 19, 1775:

> . . . How women, with heaving breasts, bravely seconded their husbands! how the countrymen, forced suddenly to arm, without guides or counsellors, took instant counsel of their courage! The mighty chorus of voices rose from the scattered farmhouses, and as it were, from the very ashes of the dead, Come forth, champions of liberty, now free your country; protect your sons and daughters, your wives and homesteads; rescue the houses of the God of your fathers, the franchises handed down from your ancestors! [44]

These heroics were the product of Bancroft's imagination. The contemporary statements of participants in that day's doings show no consciousness of the momentous character of the events. Bancroft's history distorts the facts in two ways: by indulging in rhetoric of this kind, and, as already pointed out, by allowing national prejudice to blind him to the truth as told by the sources.

Some writers embellish their narratives with picturesque but unhistorical details to make them *seem* real, and for the sake of vividness. One such might describe a home-coming of Thomas Jefferson thus: "The red disc of the sun was just sinking from view behind the western hills, and purple twilight was already gathering in the vales as Jefferson drew near to Monticello." This literary flourish might have real value if actually true to facts, but otherwise it must be classed with other untruths. Data of the kind needed to support such touches are rare in historical documents, and if nonexistent cannot be derived from the imagination. The actual arrival may have been at midnight in a pouring rain! The harmless (?) habit of distortion of this kind

[44] *Op. cit.*, IV, 154.

is so common that the critic must learn to suspect the accuracy of any statement embellished with elaborate details.

Authors whose field is the twilight zone between fiction and history frequently adopt the picturesque style to make their books interesting, and write biographies with as many intimate touches as the novelist employs in depicting the adventures and thoughts of his heroes. It is so difficult to discriminate between the imaginary and the real in such writings that the only safe course is to treat them as historical fiction, and turn elsewhere for trustworthy information.

Another common species of distortion ignores the actual sequence of events, which to be sure may be drab enough, and in order to heighten the effect presents happenings which took place at different times as if they occurred at the same moment, or experiences of separated individuals as if they happened to them as members of a company or group. During the progress of the debate over the admission of Missouri as a state, Thomas Jefferson declared that the controversy startled him "like a fire bell in the night." Unfortunately for the literary historian, the utterance was not evoked at the beginning of the controversy nor yet at its climax. The effect would be more dramatic if the historian quoted the words out of their exact historical setting—but the account would be less true as history. The "psychological moment" often passes before the actors in the human drama are aware that it has arrived.

Speakers and writers frequently distort the truth by exaggerating the intensity of their own emotions, for the purpose of exciting those of their audiences or readers. The impassioned eloquence of the orator, whether in the field of law, politics, or religion, is not the best medium for presenting facts. It is too often akin to the device of the attorney who simulates convictions which he does not hold and emotions which he does not feel, in order to win a client's cause. It is sometimes like the trick of the thief who raises the hue and cry to divert attention from himself, or that of the demagogue who slanders his opponent in order to cover his own crookedness.

iii. TESTS FOR ANONYMOUS STATEMENTS

If external criticism fails to supply data concerning author-ship, internal criticism must be directed to the *statement* instead of to the *author*. In such cases many of the tests already suggested are still applicable. It must be remembered that by authorship more is meant than the name of the writer of a document. If he has written on politics, his country, state, and party may be as important as his name, in warning the critic of his probable bias. If he has written on religion, knowledge of his creed or denomination will serve in the same way. "The Monk of St. Gall," whose name is unknown, is sufficiently identified by this appellation for many of the purposes of criticism.

Without any data on authorship the critic may still examine a statement and ask questions which will test the probability of falsehood or error: Is the statement prejudicial to the effect which the writer seems to desire to produce? An admission which diminishes the credibility of a statement which the maker wishes to have believed is an indication of truthful inten-tions.

Would falsehood be certainly detected? It is hardly to be supposed that John Smith would have published the story of his rescue by Pocahontas while she was living and certain to hear of it, unless it was true, as she would certainly have denied a false account. (It is argued that Smith knew the story was false, and avoided the denial by withholding it until after her death.) The same reasoning would apply in the case of an anonymous statement which the maker ardently desired people to believe. A difference must be recognized in the case of slanderous accusa-tions, such as those of which President Johnson was the victim. It is almost impossible to disprove such falsehoods, and mere denial is far from convincing.

Is the statement of an indifferent character? Many assertions are of such a casual or neutral nature that there is no conceivable motive for misrepresentation. If such statements are incorrect, it is due to unintentional error. The probability of error may be weighed by asking such questions as: Is the statement such that, if true, it must have been a matter of common knowledge and observation for a long time, or over a wide area? If so, the probability of error is reduced to the minimum. The same is true if the statement is such that a superficial observation would suffice for a correct report. Finally, there are statements which could never have been thought of if untrue, such as that the precepts of the Sermon on the Mount were actually proclaimed by a great teacher.

It would be impracticable to attempt to formulate questions for every possible phase of criticism. The desideratum is that the student shall cultivate a soundly critical attitude and thoughtfully adapt his procedure to the requirements of his specific problems. There is no merit in rules save as the expression of that good sense and judgment without which it is a waste of time to engage in historical studies.

3. Determinable Facts

By this time the reader may be suffering from the apprehension that it is useless to attempt to distinguish the true from the false, and may feel tempted to renounce history as a vain pursuit. Certainly there are vast numbers of statements the truth of which can never be ascertained, and the strict rules of criticism demand that all such be regarded as at best doubtful. Negative criticism raises all reasons that can be thought of for doubting; but in this way it also *removes* in many cases the grounds for doubt. Something more than this is necessary, however, to establish the truth.

Several classes of facts are regarded as ascertainable:

1. Incidental allusions in the literature of any people often reveal valuable facts concerning their customs and beliefs. Scripture references to chickens prove that, like sheep, they were common possessions of the ancient Hebrews. The collections of stories used by medieval preachers to illustrate their sermons are an important source of knowledge of the life of the

Middle Ages. Even the book of fairy tales known as the *Arabian Nights* throws much light on the customs and habits of the Mohammedans in Arabia during the reign of the great Caliph Haroun-al-Raschid.

Two cautions must be observed in interpreting such allusions. They reflect the times from which the document *dates*, but not necessarily those which it purports to describe. Moreover, one must not confound the moral or æsthetic concepts of the writer with those of the age portrayed. Penelope's fidelity to Ulysses cannot be taken as typical of the conduct of wives in ancient Greece. Nor can descriptions of objects be regarded as proof that they existed, although the author must have been acquainted with their component elements. If golden streets are mentioned, the reference proves, not that they were actually to be found anywhere, but only that the writer was familiar with both gold and streets and had a lively imagination.

2. Contemporary statements concerning customs, doctrines, and great events of any period show the existence of such customs and institutions, if they endured for a long time or over a vast space, so that they must have attracted general attention and become matters of common knowledge. However, insofar as such statements include incidental details they are subject to doubt, except where such details are of the kind discussed in the preceding paragraphs on allusions.

In this connection an explanation should be given of the fact that ancient history wears an illusory appearance of greater certainty than modern. This is because the truth concerning modern events must be found by sifting great masses of conflicting evidence while the preserved materials relating to remote times are meager. The truth is that the facts of ancient history are much more difficult to ascertain because of the dearth of independent reports.

For example, it is customary to accept the account of the early Germans by Tacitus, because it is substantially the only description extant. His statements are taken as facts, contrary to the rules of criticism, since they cannot be corroborated. It

is a case of "take it or leave it." Under such circumstances
historians commonly "take it," but their own writings should
at least hint at the difference between statements resting on
unsupported authority, and facts established by independent
witnesses. One should not state positively that it was the custom
among the early Germans to do so-and-so, but should use some
such phrase as "according to Tacitus, it was the custom," etc.
Yet on little more than the uncertain foundation which Tacitus
affords, some historians have raised elaborate theories about the
Teutonic origin of English institutions. Others have even
followed the ætiological narratives of Livy in dealing with the
earliest period of Roman history, with scarcely a suggestion of
the unsoundness of such tales as historical sources. Fortunately,
sober historians of the present day have advanced beyond this
stage.

3. The most difficult statements to deal with critically are
those which, like Tacitus' description of German customs, concern details. The statement of one person should never be
regarded as sufficient to establish the truth in such matters.
Adams recorded in his oft-mentioned diary that during the
Missouri discussion President Monroe asked the members of his
cabinet whether they regarded the pending compromise measure
as coming within the constitutional powers of Congress, and that
Calhoun was among those who answered Yes. A few years later
Calhoun was the leading champion of the contrary view, and
there is no other direct statement to corroborate that of Adams.
A cautious historian would therefore not assert as an unquestionable fact that Calhoun changed his mind; rather he would
exhibit the evidence and offer the conclusion which seemed most
probable.

There would be little risk in accepting even a newspaper
report, if contemporary, saying that the Democratic National
Nominating Convention of 1928 met at such and such a time
and place; but if the account went on to say that Mr. So-and-so
met Mr. Thus-and-so in a back room and there reached certain
important agreements concerning the nomination, corroborating

evidence would be demanded at once. If the necessary evidence could not be collected, the story would rest on a par with the charges which Beecher disseminated against Johnson.

It ofttimes happens, however, especially in recent history, that more than one statement is available with reference to particular events. All the statements are first subjected to the tests of external and internal criticism, and if they survive, are then compared and subjected to the following additional tests:

Are they (1) independent observations (2) made by different observers (3) belonging to different parties, sects, or groups (4) working under different conditions? Essential agreement in the statements of such independent witnesses will establish the truth of their statements beyond reasonable doubt. It is evident from these considerations how important it is for an investigator to collect the statements on a given point made by members of opposing groups. For example, in studying the history of a political campaign, it would be necessary to examine representative newspapers of all the parties presenting candidates.

It is to be noted that independent reports of observations are bound to differ in nonessentials, such as phraseology. Such minor variations are evidence of independence rather than error, and add to the conclusiveness of the concurrence of the accounts. *Absolute likeness would prove dependence*, and the two or more statements would be reduced to one. Where statements seem to agree, therefore, it is necessary to determine whether one has been borrowed from another, or whether they are really independent. Because Madison borrowed some of the statements which he found in the *Journal*, his papers as published seem at some points to confirm the *Journal*, whereas in fact the statements rest solely upon its authority.

On the other hand, where statements seem contradictory, it is necessary to determine whether the contradiction is real or only apparent; they may bear upon different aspects of the same matter. The six blind men who went to see the elephant did not really contradict one another in their varying reports. Nor did they corroborate one another.

No conclusion can be reached where statements of equal intrinsic credibility are really contradictory. An example of such contradiction is found in the statements made by eye-witnesses concerning the firing of the first shot at Lexington. Nor can a conclusion be reached where statements deal with different aspects of a matter, for this is equivalent to dealing with different subjects.

Both Adams and Jefferson were members of the committee appointed by Congress in 1776 to draft the Declaration of Independence. Each gave an account of the drafting, written about a half-century later, and these accounts do not entirely agree. Adams relates that the committee met and appointed a subcommittee, consisting of Jefferson and himself, to make the draft; and moreover, that he persuaded Jefferson to do the drafting. When Jefferson had done so, according to Adams the draft was reported to the main committee and accepted substantially without change.

Jefferson denied that there had been a subcommittee, and asserted that he consulted Franklin as well as Adams, and that they made several changes in the draft, as the original paper still showed. These corrections, he said were supported by written notes which he had made on the spot at the time.

In these accounts there is both essential agreement at certain points and contradiction at others. Consequently they establish certain facts and leave other points undetermined. That Jefferson drew the draft is clear, and also that he consulted Adams. Whether there was a subcommittee is uncertain: Adams may, as Jefferson said, have "misremembered" informal conferences as meetings of a subcommittee, while Jefferson may have forgotten the subcommittee because he consulted Franklin as well as Adams. His written memorandum is inconclusive of the point, for it merely says that "The Committee for drawing the Declaration of Independence desired me to do it. It was accordingly done." Adams's statement about changes is contradicted by Jefferson, and the latter's assertions are confirmed by the appearance of the document but not by the memorandum.[45]

4. Statements which are not directly confirmed by independent assertions may gain credibility if they are found to fit in harmoniously with other facts which are known. That Calhoun changed his mind with reference to the powers of Congress over slavery in the territories seems likely because he changed it on other matters. At the time of the contest over Missouri he was known to be an extreme nationalist in his views regarding the powers of Congress; while before the close of the thirties he had become as pronounced an advocate of the strict construction of those powers. Such facts render the truth of Adams's diary record quite probable.

Another example: Some one asserts that Andrew Jackson's opposition to the administration of Adams was due to his belief that Adams had won the Presidency in the House election of 1825 through a corrupt bargain with Henry Clay. Jackson himself never gave this explanation, nor was it made for him by any authorized spokesman. Yet it is probably true, for the following reasons: It is known that Jackson greeted Adams cordially on the day of the latter's inauguration, and showed no resentment over his own defeat. It had already been charged that Adams had made a bargain with Clay, promising him an appointment in return for his support in the House election. Jackson knew of this charge, but his conduct at the inauguration indicates that he did not believe it. When a few days later, Adams nominated Clay as Secretary of State, Jackson began immediately to assert that he had been robbed of the Presidency by the "Judas of the West." The inference is almost inescapable that the appointment of Clay convinced him that the pre-election charge was true, and that he consequently became hostile to an administration which he might otherwise have judged according to its measures.

[45] *Cf.* presentation of this problem in Henry Johnson, *Teaching of History in Elementary and Secondary Schools* (The Macmillan Company, New York, 1926), 432–434.

4. Types of Discredited Statements

Certain types of statements cannot be accepted by historians even when they are made by numerous alleged eye-witnesses. Most prominent among these are assertions which are in discord with scientific knowledge. It must be recalled that every statement, before it can be accepted, must be found to rest upon reliable observation. If the report conflicts with the teachings which science bases upon observation, the historian cannot do otherwise than hold that the observation on which the report rests has been faulty. Such reports of supposed observations are attributed to ignorance, illusions, or hallucinations.

This attitude of the historian is not a denial of the possibility of miracles, but *for his purposes* accounts of them are no more usable than if they were proved to be untrue. Whatever reasons there may be for believing them fall outside of the critical categories which he is able to employ. With the progress of science it sometimes becomes evident that statements which seemed scientifically impossible are not impossible at all. On the basis of his own observations a dweller in the equatorial regions might be warranted in denying that water could take a solid form unless by a miracle. Wider knowledge would reduce this miraculous occurrence to a commonplace.

Every statement which is in discord with the body of (supposedly) known historical facts must be regarded as improbable, although open-mindedness requires that the body of supposed facts be held subject to revision whenever adequate evidence is forthcoming. Such revision is, of course, constantly taking place.

5. Illustrative Problem

In practice, the effort to ascertain the facts in any particular case requires the application of a combination of tests specially selected from those which have been discussed, because of their fitness for the special problems involved. As a last study in critical method, let us examine an illustration of this final proposition.

A well-known college textbook on American history, in referring to the part played by the New York delegation in the House election of 1825, says that Van Buren

> hoped the state's vote would remain divided on the first ballot. Thus there would be no choice on that ballot, which would give him opportunity at a later time to cast the New York vote for Adams and secure for himself the honor of president-maker.[46]

Now it would be unreasonable to require that the writer of a textbook make no statement without first-hand examination and criticism of all available sources. The scope of a textbook is so inclusive that while it may in part reflect the author's own scholarship, it must be largely a summary of standard authorities. In other words, the author cannot conform to the rules which legitimately apply to the writer of a monograph. The consequence is that all textbooks contain numerous erroneous statements which are repeated by writer after writer until some critical investigator brings the facts to light, and passes on his conclusions to the text writers. By this process old errors are being constantly corrected, but the perfecting of texts proceeds slowly.

To return to the quotation: No critical writer would repeat this statement about Van Buren on the authority of a textbook without testing it. The book does not indicate the source of the information, but the critic would institute a search for the original author. If his bibliographical information was broad or his methods of running down clues shrewd, he would ere long find the following passage in Hammond's *Political History of New York:*

> I have it from the best authority that Mr. Van Buren and his most immediate friends of the Crawford party meant, at the next balloting to have given Adams the election. They wished to have had it in their power to have said to Mr. Adams, "your friends and Mr. Clay's cannot make you president—We give you the office." [47]

[46] John Spencer Bassett, *A Short History of the United States* (The Macmillan Company, New York, 1913), 380.

[47] Jabez D. Hammond, *The History of Political Parties in the State of New York from the Ratification of the Constitution to December, 1840* (4th edn., Phinney & Co., Buffalo, 1850), II, 190.

This statement bears evidence of being the source of the assertion in the textbook, although there is no certainty that Bassett, the writer, drew directly from Hammond. Once in circulation an error displays great vitality. More than sixty years before the publication of Bassett's textbook, Hammond himself had corrected the assertion about Van Buren. This correction appears in a note in the Appendix of the fourth edition of the *Political History*, and reads as follows:

> I have ascertained that the statement in the text is materially incorrect. I have lately been informed from unquestionable authority, that shortly before the election of the President, a meeting was held by the members of the New York delegation, friendly to the election of Mr. Crawford, at which, upon a full view of the subject, they decided with great unanimity, to adhere to Mr. Crawford to the end, and leave the election to be made by others. I have this statement from a gentleman of high standing who was then a member of Congress, and was present at the caucus. It is, however, due to myself to add that I had the best reasons and high authority for the allegations contained in the text. I was at Washington at the time of the election, and was in favor of the election of Mr. Adams. From various conversations which were held in my presence with the Crawford members from this state, *some days before the election*, I was led to believe that on the second ballot they would vote for Mr. Adams. But I did not assert the fact on such grounds. In the year 1841, I was told by a leading and impartial friend of Mr. Adams, then a member of the House of Representatives, that *he knew the fact*, that the Crawford members from this state would after the first ballot have voted for Mr. Adams. . . . Some time before the election several of Mr. Crawford's friends had assured him that such would be their course, and he had never been informed of the caucus I have mentioned where the persons with whom he conversed changed their determination. My friend did not intend to deceive me, but was himself deceived. . . .[48]

Another important document bears upon this problem of the part of Van Buren and his colleagues in this election. This is Van Buren's autobiography, which was written about the middle of the nineteenth century, some years after the publication of

[48] Hammond, *op. cit.*, Note C, p. 540.

the first edition of Hammond's book, but not published until the present century. Van Buren had seen an early edition of Hammond's work, but not the one in which he made the correction which has been quoted. In regard to the House election Van Buren wrote:

> I obtained a meeting of the friends of Crawford in the New York delegation and proposed to them in a few remarks that we should abstain to the end from taking a part in favor of either of the three [other two] gentlemen returned to the House—Jackson, Adams or Clay. [Van Buren writing from memory is in error here, as Clay's name was not before the House, but only those of Jackson, Adams, and Crawford.] I assured them that there was no danger that an election would not be made by others and that if the friends of Mr. Crawford stood aloof from the intrigues which such a contest would produce unavoidably they would form a nucleus around which the old Republicans of the Union might rally if the new Administration did not act upon their principles as we apprehended would be the case. They resolved with perfect unanimity to pursue that course, and I do not believe that a single individual of our number ever thought of departing from it: certainly not one did so depart. Judge Hammond was therefore misinformed in regard to their intention to vote in any event [that is, if the first ballot did not result in a choice] for Mr. Adams.[49]

Reviewing all this evidence, the critic reaches the following conclusions: Bassett's second-hand statement must be put aside at once. There is an apparent contradiction between Hammond's assertion that Van Buren and his friends intended to support Adams after the first ballot and Van Buren's account of the caucus agreement to vote for Crawford to the end, but this contradiction proves not to be real. Hammond appears in the rôle of an impartial but not very critical historian, whose reliance upon unnamed authorities is not very reassuring. His corrected statement agrees with Van Buren's, but the "unquestionable authority" on which it rests is not identified. The original statement had likewise rested on "the best authority"; and it is conceivable that his "unquestionable authority" for the

---

[49] *The Autobiography of Martin Van Buren*, edited by John C. Fitzpatrick (American Historical Association *Annual Report* for 1918, II), 149–150.

revision was Van Buren himself. In that case there is only one authority for the alleged caucus agreement, and that authority is a man who had a personal interest in having his statement believed, and whose memory shows signs of failure.

That Van Buren was Hammond's authority seems unlikely, however, since the autobiography neither hints at an effort to bring about a correction nor reveals any knowledge that one had been or would be made. Nevertheless some doubt remains about the correctness of the "correction." But conceding Hammond's limitations, the evidence is fairly conclusive that there was *at one time* a disposition on the part of Crawford's friends to switch their ballots to Adams after the first ballot. According to Hammond, conversations in his presence in 1825 showed this intention, and a friend of Adams assured him in 1841 that he knew of this intention at the time. The assumption that there was such a plan fits in with Van Buren's account of the calling of a caucus, by supplying a motive for calling it, and adds to the probability that Van Buren wished to bring about a change of mind. Van Buren's testimony thus confirms rather than contradicts Hammond's original statement that the Crawford men intended to vote for Adams on the second ballot. Nor does Van Buren's statement that they changed their minds contradict the statements made to Hammond on which he based his original assertion, for it relates to another phase of the matter. Events throw no light on what the Crawford men would have done on a second ballot, as the first resulted in Adams's election.

A beginner would find it a good exercise to make a formal analysis of the evidence in a problem such as this, along the following lines:

1. What are Bassett's statements?
   Answer:
   a. Crawford men in New York delegation intended to abandon him after first ballot and vote for Adams.
   b. Van Buren, as leader, made this plan hoping to secure for himself the honor of president-maker.

2. What value attaches to Bassett's statements?
Answer: No more than attaches to those of his source.

3. Who is his authority?
Answer: Not named. Probably Hammond.

4. What are Hammond's statements?
Answer:
   a. Some Crawford men, including Van Buren, intended to vote for Adams on second ballot.
   b. "They" wished to have the honor of deciding the election.

5. Does Hammond make these statements as his own observations?
Answer: Partly.

6. What is their basis?
Answer:
   a. Various conversations of Crawford men from New York, in his presence, some days before election, revealed intention to vote for Adams on second ballot.
   b. In 1841 a friend of Adams told him he knew of this intention, as Crawford men had assured him of it some time before the election.

7. Do these statements warrant the allegations in the text of Hammond?
Answer:
   a. They support the first statement.
   b. They do not warrant the statement as to motive. It is a mere surmise and must be dismissed.

8. Are there any statements which seem to contradict Hammond's first allegation?
Answer:
   a. An unknown authority mentioned by Hammond in Note C.
   b. Van Buren's autobiography.

9. What do they say?
Answer: A caucus was held at which the Crawford men resolved to adhere to him to the end.

10. Is there any indication in Hammond's statements that the Crawford men intended to vote for Adams on the second ballot in spite of the caucus?
Answer: No.

11. Does Van Buren deny that Crawford men had planned to switch to Adams?
Answer: No.

12. Is there then any real contradiction in the several statements?
Answer: No. They concern different matters.

13. To what do the statements reduce?
Answer:
   a. Hammond: Some Crawford men indicated an intention of supporting Adams on the second ballot, but
   b. At a caucus they decided to adhere to Crawford to the end.
   c. Van Buren: I called a caucus and proposed that the Crawford men should stick to him to the end. This was agreed to.

14. What of the probable truth of these statements?
Answer:
   a. Hammond is a semiexpert investigator. His first statement rests upon observations of more than one witness to whom he listened, and is probably true.
   b. Van Buren's statement may be questioned on several grounds:
      1) It was made long after the event, and betrays lapses of memory.
      2) He was personally interested as his reputation was more or less at stake.
      3) It is supported only by the testimony of an unnamed person, mentioned by Hammond, who may have been Van Buren himself.
   c. On the other hand:
      1) If the unnamed authority was Van Buren, his autobiography might be expected to give some hint of the fact.
      2) If it was rumored that the Crawford men were planning to switch to Adams, Van Buren would have had a reason for calling a caucus *if he opposed* the plan. His statement fits in with Hammond's first.
   d. Van Buren's statement is not certainly but yet quite probably true.

After such an analysis, a historian, say a textbook writer, who wished merely to give his conclusions without troubling his readers by reviewing the evidence, would write somewhat as follows:

According to the available evidence, Crawford's friends in the New York delegation manifested a disposition to switch their votes to Adams after the first ballot. Van Buren, however, declared many years later that he had opposed this course, and that in a caucus of the Crawford men in the delegation it had been decided

to support Crawford to the end. As Adams was elected on the
first ballot, and Van Buren's statement lacks adequate corrobora-
tion, it remains somewhat uncertain what course the New York
men would have followed in the event of further balloting.
Certainly there is no sufficient warrant for the assertion sometimes
made that Van Buren was scheming to pose as president-maker,
by throwing the decisive weight into the scales in favor of Adams
on the second ballot.

III. HISTORICAL COMPOSITION

1. THE WORKING OUTLINE

By the time an investigator has collected his material, a clearly defined outline of his theme should have taken shape in his mind. As has already been said, the evolution of the outline should keep pace with the gathering of data, and with the completion of the collecting the arrangement of the data should have been brought into close conformity with the plan of presentation in the monograph. However, before beginning to write it is advisable to set down the outline in black and white. It will then serve as a guide in writing, and in perfected form will become the analytical table of contents which the completed monograph should include. Moreover, working it out will encourage a thoughtful review of the whole body of material, which should yield the following excellent fruits: (1) mastery of the data; (2) clear perception of the relations of parts of the theme to the whole; (3) certainty that sound conclusions have been reached on all problems; (4) clear definition of objectives. No writer should put pen to paper until he knows what he can do with his material, and such a review and outline are essential preliminaries of rapid and accurate writing. With such preparation the actual effort at expression in fitting language will also help to clarify ideas still further.

The working outline should be an analysis of the proposed contents of the text. It should be divided in a logical way into main and subordinate parts. Each main division should possess either a topical or chronological unity of its own, and the subdivisions should form a logical outline of the topic covered in that portion of the study to which they belong.[1] The plan of the outline must be determined by the nature of the materials as

[1] The Table of Contents of this manual may be examined as an illustration.

revealed by this review, and in turn the materials should be given their final arrangement, in the order of the divisions of the outline. Further changes in the outline and in the arrangement of the data may result from the new insight which should come with the effort to present the theme, and hence the final table of contents may show some improvement over the working outline.

2. The Preliminary Draft

If these suggestions are followed the step from outline to first draft should be an easy one. The outline may be regarded as a skeleton, and the notes, arranged on the same plan, as the flesh. The preliminary draft should put the flesh on the bones; to do this a writing out of the essentials contained in the notes is required.

Even a first draft should be more than a series of quotations. The novice sometimes misconceives the task of composition as a mere putting together of quoted passages, as beads are strung. For the most part, careful paraphrases are preferable to long quotations. The use of the gist of the statements of others in the student's own words permits him to display his powers of interpretation, criticism, and presentation to better advantage, and is conducive to a more flexible and graceful style. His own words are needed especially to introduce quotations; to state the substance of long passages from sources or other writers, so that the words actually quoted may be limited to those containing the pith of the passage; to explain quoted passages; and to bridge over gracefully from one quotation to another.

When quotations are resorted to, an effort should be made to vary the introductory phrases. If one is preceded by the words Said he: in the next, a phrase may be interjected at the first natural break in the quotation, thus: "I shall never believe," wrote Washington, "that . . .," etc. A quotation of six lines or more is often printed in smaller type than the text, and sometimes when so printed the quotation marks are omitted.[2] On the

[2] See pages 84, 95, et passim.

typewriter a similar effect can be produced by using double spacing for the text and single spacing for the quoted passage. The contrast between text and quotation can be further emphasized by slightly shortening the quoted lines. The words used to introduce the quotation should be a part of the paragraph which precedes it.

To compose a monograph largely of quotations would be equivalent to setting raw materials before the reader. If this only were done the writer would stand convicted of having neglected the critical work by which facts are obtained from statements and made the basis of interpretations and conclusions. Often, it is true, a scientific writer finds it desirable to exhibit some of the raw materials, in order to make evident the critical use which has been made of them, and to show that the conclusions arrived at are valid. But he dare not stop with a display of raw materials without such use of them, leaving the reader to do his own critical work and draw his own conclusions.

The writer should make a conscious and deliberate effort to free his own statements from all the influences—prejudice, ignorance, negligence, emotion, excitement, etc.—which he has learned to regard as tending to warp the statements which compose his raw material: he must apply to his own statements the same rigid critical tests which he has practiced upon his sources.

The prime purpose of the preliminary draft is to mobilize every essential of narration, exposition, argument, and conclusion, fully, clearly, and accurately. Into the draft should be brought all of the facts which are to enter into the completed monograph. It must be remembered that facts are of various kinds or orders. An event is a fact of one kind. If an opinion or belief has been held, whether it is true or false, *that it has been held* is a fact of another kind. Much history has been made by the fact that people held false beliefs. The presidential election of 1828 was probably decided by the erroneous conviction of many voters that Adams had won office in 1825 by means of a bargain with Clay.

An institution is a fact; a relationship between facts is a fact. Sound generalizations are facts. The writer who confines his production to a mere narrative of events, void of interpretations based upon the perception of relationships, turns out a barren story, mere annals or chronicles. In a small way, the Illustrative Problem in the preceding division of this manual exemplifies the way in which data should be handled for interpretative history. Such history, while vastly more difficult to write, and proportionately liable to error when attempted by second-rate intellects, is also vastly more worth while if a writer has real ability.

While making this draft little heed need be paid to literary quality. It is easy for persons with strong literary impulses to waste time in polishing the first few paragraphs, but the temptation to do this should be resisted. When the substance has once been committed to writing, a revision of the literary form will be possible with a minimum of effort. If the writer is a graduate student, his work should not be submitted for criticism until it has been given the final literary touches—unless he is prepared to be misjudged, or unless the director of his work desires to examine the draft solely with reference to contents. Especially should the adviser not be asked to read each chapter piecemeal. The student should do his best to turn out a good piece of work by independent effort.

It is essential, nevertheless, to develop the draft with careful attention to the logical sequence of ideas and topics. It is helpful to remember also that in presenting matter to readers one should proceed from what is presumably known by them to that which presumably the monograph will add to their knowledge. A scientific writer proceeds from the general to the specific, the general being already common knowledge and affording the setting for the specific, which is the writer's new contribution. Concretely, a historical writer must give his special theme its proper historical setting, not merely in a formal introduction at the beginning of the book, but at every stage where it is required for clearness and symmetry.

3. Forms

The rules governing the forms employed in historical writing do not fall in that immutable class to which the laws of the Medes and Persians are supposed to belong. In fact, there is a wide variation in the practice of writers, as anyone may discover by the most superficial observation. It would be fortunate, for reasons of convenience, if historical writers as a class could agree upon a uniform code of rules. In the absence of such agreement every one is at liberty to pursue his own course, provided only that his practices are reasonable, consistent, and effective.

It seems, nevertheless, that good judgment should lead beginners to follow the practices of the American Historical Association, the Mississippi Valley Historical Association, and other prominent organizations of the fraternity in the United States, as exemplified in their publications.[3] The forms explained herein are based on these models. The student's patience will be less taxed if he can perceive that there is a rational purpose governing each detail of these practices, or of any good alternative code.

a. *Footnotes*

As a part of the task of making the preliminary draft, the footnotes and bibliography should be put in proper form. If directions already given have been carefully followed, it will now be comparatively easy to master the additional technique.

i. Purposes and Usage

Footnotes are used for several purposes: (1) to cite the authority for or source of statements in the text; (2) to relieve the text of matter which interrupts its flow and tends to lessen its interest, such as technical discussions and incidental com-

---

[3] Many publishers issue style books for the guidance of untrained writers. They are usually willing, however, to conform to the wishes of authors who have a well-defined system of their own.

ments;[4] (3) to cite other discussions or additional information upon topics in the text;[5] and (4) to give cross references.[6]

The first of the uses mentioned demands some further explanation. It is due to the acceptance by contemporary historians of the view that a historical monograph is a scientific product. The laboratory experiments performed by one scientist may be repeated by another as a check upon the results reported. Just so the authorities upon which the conclusions in a monograph rest may be used by other critical students to check these conclusions. The broad rule emerges that a monograph writer should *cite his authority or source for every fact, opinion, or conclusion* (save his own) *stated in the text*.

This rule does not apply merely, as some suppose, where the words of another are quoted verbatim. Of course the source of a quotation must be indicated; but a citation is just as necessary when words are paraphrased or the substance only is given. It must be remembered that most of the data which a historical writer uses are not his at first hand, but are derived; his own opinions, conclusions, and interpretations are the only original contributions he can make.

This fundamental rule is subject to one exception: background facts, the common facts of general history which it may be assumed every intelligent reader knows, require no citations.[7]

While it is essential that the source of each derived statement be made clear, it is not always necessary to give a separate reference for each. Where several facts or alleged facts drawn from the same source are presented consecutively, it is permissible to cite the source but once, at the conclusion of the paragraph, or series of paragraphs, if the continuity of the

[4] For illustrations see notes on pages 9, 13, 17, *et passim.*
[5] As is done on pages 7, 58, 63, *et passim.*
[6] *Cf.* pages 20, 25, 46, *et passim.*
[7] Such facts should not be omitted, since to deprive the theme of its setting mars the symmetry of the presentation. Besides many readers need to have common historical facts brought to mind by a review, in order to grasp the relations of the special study to general history and to appreciate the contribution which the study makes.

passage is clear to the eye.[8] If there is any room for the reader to doubt that all of the statements are derived from the same source, the citation should not be deferred beyond the end of the first paragraph, with additional citations at the close of each of the series. It is better to err on the side of too many citations than to give too few.

An alternative where a series of paragraphs condense a single authority is to indicate this fact in the initial note.[9] Further references may then be dispensed with. A critical writer, however, will seldom be content to rely upon a single account; hence occasions for notes in this blanket form should be infrequent.

It must also be remembered that the purpose of a citation is to indicate the source to which the writer is *indebted*, whether it be the primary source or not. If the investigator obtains data from an author who quotes a document or another writer, the investigator's authority is the work *consulted*, not the one to which it refers. The dangers of second-hand information have been discussed in the section on criticism. Scholarly work demands first-hand use of sources. But if a secondary writer quotes a source and the monographist relies upon the secondary writer for a knowledge of the source, he takes the risk of error and should be honest enough to admit it. It is a species of dishonesty to cite a source known only through a secondary work, without indicating that fact by the form used in the citation.

It should be obvious that to cite a secondary statement based on a particular source, in addition to citing the source, does not strengthen the citation, unless the secondary statement includes a judgment or interpretation. Nor does citation of two or more secondary statements of an alleged fact derived from the same source add to the probability of its truthfulness or strengthen a statement in the text repeating it. Yet such citations are not uncommon in the work of novices. A thorough appreciation of the principles of criticism will prevent such crudities.

---

[8] For an example see pages 84, 85.
[9] A statement may be made in the note to this effect: "In this narrative of . . . the writer has followed the account by. . . ."

If a magazine article has been used, the article, not the magazine, is the authority, the latter being mentioned only to show where the article may be found. If a book used belongs in a series, the authority is the particular volume, not the series; in fact, the authority is the particular statement in the book which is cited to support the text. In a similar way, a collection of source material cannot be an authority. For a specific fact or statement a writer's authority is never a collection, but some particular document reprinted in it, such as a letter or speech. In a citation the document should be both identified and located.

ii. ILLUSTRATIONS OF USAGE

The text and footnotes in the preceding pages of this manual are intended to afford illustrations of usage. They should be examined in connection with the following explanations:

1. The index figures used in the text to call attention to footnotes should be elevated slightly above the type line, both when printed and when typewritten. The corresponding figures in the footnotes should be elevated in the same way and set slightly to the right of the margin of the page, with no space between the figures and the words which follow.

2. Notes should be numbered consecutively through each chapter or main division, beginning with 1 in each, unless the total number in the study is less than 100, in which case the numbering may run consecutively throughout the work.

3. The index figures should never be placed at the beginning of a paragraph, title, sentence, or quoted passage. Their normal position is at the close of the sentence which contains the statement requiring a citation. If the sentence requires more than one, the figures should be placed at the appropriate points within the sentence, unless the reference cites two or more authorities for the same statement. In that case they should be placed in one footnote with a semicolon to separate them.

4. In footnotes, the number of a volume should be given in capital Roman numerals, and page numbers in Arabic figures. Lower case Roman numerals should be used in citing pages of

introductions and other preliminary portions of books, if they are used in the books, as is the case in this manual.

5. The words *volume* and *page*, and their abbreviations, are not necessary if the foregoing directions are observed, except in cases where the figures might be misunderstood to stand for something else. A reference to a chapter number usually requires the use of the abbreviation chap. or ch., since the numerals following might otherwise be mistaken for volume or page references. Chapter numbers are usually given in capital Roman numerals.

6. If a monograph is without a bibliography, the bibliographical data for works cited must be given in the first footnote in which reference is made to them. To illustrate this practice, certain notes have been drawn in the preceding pages in the form which would be proper if the manual contained no bibliography.[10]

Such matter is really engrafted upon the footnote. Its essential purpose is different, *viz.*, to support a specific statement by a particular citation. The purpose of a bibliography, on the other hand, is to describe in their entirety works which are referred to. The bibliography gives its descriptions once for all; the notes refer to each authority as often as may be necessary— that is, every time a statement needs support. The functions do not naturally blend; hence a monograph should always contain a formal bibliography, and matter of that kind should be kept out of the notes. If an article is prepared for publication in a journal, however, there is usually no alternative: the bibliography must be dispensed with and data of that nature must be included in the footnotes.

7. To avoid the repetition of long titles, writers employ the word *ibid.* (abbreviated form of the Latin *ibidem*, meaning *the same*). When this term stands alone it takes the place of author's name, title of book, and volume and page indications— in fact, it is equivalent to ditto marks. If a different page or volume is intended, the proper numerals must of course be added. *Ibid.* always refers to the work last cited. If its use

[10] See pages 63, 66, 70, 74, 88–90, 92, 103, 105, 107.

requires the turning of pages to identify this work, it is better to use an abbreviated form of title, with the author's name, omitting initials.[11] If a work is to be cited frequently, it is well, in the first note mentioning it, after giving the full form, to indicate the short form by which it will be cited in later references.[12]

8. When a work has been once cited and other references have intervened before it is again referred to, *op. cit.* (from the Latin *opere citato, in the work cited*) may be used in place of the title. The author's name must be repeated when *op. cit.* is used, since otherwise the "work cited" cannot be identified.

One should not employ a short title for a work at one time and use *op. cit.* at another. One or the other form should be adhered to. The frequent use of *op. cit.* smacks of pedantry, especially where the same work is referred to frequently. Shortened title forms are perhaps generally preferable; indeed, some writers think that it is sufficient to use merely the author's name in all citations after the first. But neither this very informal practice nor the use of *op. cit.* has the flexibility of the abbreviated form. If an author has written more than one book on the same subject and these are cited by another, neither *op. cit.* nor the author's name is sufficient to distinguish them.

9. If a writer's name is introduced into the text, it need not be repeated in the note.[13] Likewise, if the title of a book is given in the text it need not be repeated in the note. But the use of names of authors and titles of books in the text is to be deprecated. Citations belong in the notes, except when the author or title is an essential part of the discussion. If the identity of the authority is of no particular consequence to the reader in following the thought, it is better to use vague phrases, such as "one author holds," or "according to a prominent authority," thus emphasizing the idea which is being presented to the reader and avoiding the distraction of his attention by the mention of a name which introduces an irrelevant factor. It is better still,

[11] For examples, see pages 58, 60, 68, 83, 85.   [13] See pages 44, 45, 75, 95.
[12] See pages 68, 77.

so far as possible, to tell the story in the text without intruding the thought of authorities, leaving that matter to the footnotes.

10. When a passage is quoted in a footnote the citation for it should follow, not precede.[14] When a work not listed in the bibliography is cited in a footnote with bibliographical data included such data should be interpolated in parentheses between the title of the volume and the page figures.[15] If the footnote is purely bibliographical and is without volume or page references, the marks of parenthesis may be omitted.[16] The form is then substantially what it would be in a bibliography except that the author's given name precedes the family name.[17]

11. The name of an author should not be used in the possessive case when preceding the title in a footnote. This rule does not hold when they are introduced into the text.[18]

12. A citation of a magazine article followed immediately by a second citation of the same article calls for the use of *ibid.* in the second citation. If other citations intervene, *loc. cit.* (Latin *loco citato, in the place cited*), is used instead of *op. cit.* when the article is again mentioned. The writer's name must be repeated when *loc. cit.* is used.[19]

13. Some usages of which the text and notes of the manual do not afford examples remain to be explained. If a writer uses information which another author has drawn from a newspaper which he cites, the note of the former gives credit to his secondary authority, but may mention his source of information, thus:

> Dewey, op. cit., 307, citing Public Opinion, issue of October 17, 1895.

The form of this note may be reversed, so that it will read: *Public Opinion*, October 17, 1895, cited by Dewey, *op. cit.*, 307. These forms should not be regarded as interchangeable;

[14] See pages 3, 66.
[15] See pages 88–90.
[16] See page 71, n. 16.
[17] *Ibid.*
[18] See pages 18, 23, 24.
[19] See pages 74, 77.

that is, the writer should adopt one or the other and adhere to it. Either means that he has not examined the issue of *Public Opinion*, but has relied on Dewey. If the newspaper is consulted the secondary reference drops out. Page and column references are useful in citing newspapers but are commonly omitted. Editorials or other special classes of items in newspapers should be distinguished thus:

> Editorial in New York Evening Post, Jan. 17, 1907.
> Associated Press Dispatch, Chicago Tribune, Aug. 11, 1914.

If a statement rests upon a document contained in a collection, the document should be cited, not merely the collection. A subsequent citation follows the form for a periodical article, *ibid.* or *loc. cit.* being used depending on whether there has been an intermediate citation:

> Letter of George Washington to Alexander Hamilton, July 10, 1787, in Farrand, Records, III, 56–57.
> Hamilton to John Jay, Aug. 4, 1787. Ibid., 75.
> Washington, loc. cit.

If the name of the letter writer is brought into the text it need not be repeated in the note. Thus if the text reads: " 'Influence is no government,' said Washington, commenting on the failure of the Articles of Confederation," the footnote should read:

> Letter to Henry Lee, October 31, 1786. W. C. Ford, The Writings of George Washington, XI, 76 et seq.

References to books which belong in series should cite the particular volume used, but its place in the series should be indicated:

> J. H. Latané, America as a World Power, 1897–1907 (volume XXV of The American Nation, ed. by A. B. Hart), 232.

An essay in a composite volume is cited like a periodical article.[a] A decision of the Supreme Court should be cited by name of the case and its location in the reports.[bc] Proceedings in Congress are cited by giving the title of the series containing the record, the number of the Congress and session, and the page or column numbers.[d] Examples:

[a] Carl Becker, "Kansas." Turner Essays in American History, 85–111.

[b] Marbury v. Madison, 1 Cranch, 137.

[c] De Lima v. Bidwell, 182 U. S., 1.

[d] Annals of Congress, 5 Cong., 1 sess., 75–140. (In subsequent references the title may be abbreviated to Annals, or Ann. of Cong.)

The statutes are cited without name of editor or compiler. Government documents are designated in many ways. In some cases they have titles and bear the names of authors, editors, or compilers. Sometimes they carry the name of a commission, committee, department, or bureau which is in a sense the author or at least the sponsor for them. Data of these kinds should be included in the citations, just as in the case of books. In the case of well-known and much-used compilations it is not necessary to include documentary description.

Examples:

U. S. Stat. at Large, I, 76–84.

Joseph F. Johnson, The Canadian Banking System. U. S. National Monetary Commission Publications. 61 Cong., 2 sess., Sen. Doc. 583.

Kappler, Indian Affairs, I, 45.

The italics used in the title on the Canadian Banking System mean that the item fills the volume in the documents (cf. page 18). Some documents, like composite books, contain several items. If that were the case here, the title of the part— "The Canadian Banking System"—would be inclosed in quotation marks, and only the title of the document (Sen. Doc. 583) would be in italics. References to essays or articles in reports, annuals, and studies issued by learned organizations follow the same rules (see page 18).

Logan Esarey, "The Organization of the Jacksonian Party in Indiana." Miss. Valley Histl. Assn. Proceedings for 1913–1914, 220–243; W. F. Gephart, Transportation and Industrial Development in the Middle West. Columbia University Studies, XXXIV.

iii. ABBREVIATIONS

In addition to the Latin terms which have already been explained (*sic.*, *ibid.*, *op. cit.*, and *loc. cit.*), the following are in frequent use and many of them will be found in the foregoing pages: *cf.* (*confer*), compare (used to direct attention to another passage or statement, in the same book or elsewhere); *e.g.* (*exempli gratia*), for example; *et al.* (*et alii*), and others; *et seq.* (*et sequentes*), and following (used to indicate that the matter referred to is found on pages beginning with the one cited and continuing rather indefinitely); [20] *i.e.* (*id est*), that is; *et passim*, and here and there (used to indicate that matter referred to is not found within definite page limits in the work cited, but is scattered about); *ante*, before (used with page number as a cross reference to call attention to something in a preceding chapter of the book); *post*, after (used like *ante*, but referring to matter in a subsequent chapter); *supra*, above (used for cross reference to any preceding matter); *infra*, below (used for cross reference to any subsequent matter); *q.v.* (*quod vide*), which see (a direction to look up the subject mentioned); *n.*, note (sometimes used in the combination *f.n.*, footnote); *vide*, see (used in cross references, or like *cf.*); *viz.*, namely.

It is a rule that foreign words and phrases should be printed in italics. By attraction, it would seem, English abbreviations associated with the above Latin derivatives are often italicized. Abbreviations are particularly useful in footnotes, but should be used sparingly in the text, and only for well considered reasons.

Explanations of the foregoing list of foreign terms, as well as abbreviations of English words, will be found in any good dictionary.

b. *Bibliography: Classification, Function, and Usage*

A bibliography is a formal list of materials relating to a particular subject. In a typical monograph the bibliography is a list of the authorities, both source and secondary, cited in the footnotes. Sometimes it is extended to embrace materials not

---

[20] The form *ff.* is sometimes used with the same meaning as *et seq.*, but its derivation is irregular and it is hardly in good standing.

used in writing the monograph, in order that it may be complete for the subject. In writings of certain types, on the other hand, it may not include all works cited in the footnotes, but may be restricted to a particular class. (*Cf.* the present volume.)

In a scholarly work the bibliography is often annotated; that is, each entry is followed by a comment evaluating the item with relation to the subject of the study. Annotated bibliographies are often required in the case of essays submitted in prize competitions, such as those of the American Historical Association.

The items in every bibliography should be classified; that is, they should be arranged in groups according to their character. The broad distinction between sources and secondary writings, or primary and secondary sources, as they are sometimes called, although ofttimes used as the basis of classification, is not entirely satisfactory, if there is no further segregation of items according to their nature. Probably no two bibliographies can be classified on exactly the same plan, because the character of the materials and their grouping varies with the subject and purpose. The form here submitted may be taken as a model in a general way, subject to such modification as may be needed to adapt it to each specific study: [21]

1. Manuscript Materials.
2. Government Publications:
   a. Federal.
   b. State.
   c. Local.
3. Newspapers.
4. Biographies, Memoirs, and Writings of Public Men.
5. Other Primary Sources.
6. General Histories.
7. Special Monographs.
8. Articles and Essays in Periodicals, Annuals, and Publications of Learned Societies.
9. Miscellaneous.

The function of the bibliography should be clearly distinguished from that of footnotes. The latter are used to cite

[21] *Cf.* Bibliography on page 143, *et seq.*

authority for specific statements; they designate the exact place where the authoritative utterance is to be found. The former *describe the works* in which the data cited in notes are to be found. Thus a footnote tells the reader that a particular statement by Thomas Jefferson was made in a letter written to John Adams on a certain day, and that this letter is published in a certain volume of a certain edition of Jefferson's writings, and on a certain page. A bibliographical entry is not concerned with this letter, nor with any particular page or volume of Jefferson's works, even though there be but one citation of his works in the entire monograph. Its purpose is to inform the reader that the edition of the works of Jefferson which has been cited was edited by So-and-so, and published in so many volumes, by such and such a publisher, in such and such a place, in certain years.

The notes and bibliography are therefore supplementary; the reader who desires to look up a reference which he finds in a footnote must turn to the bibliography to find a full description of the work in which the letter or document is printed.

The relations between footnotes and bibliography, and the importance of the data which each supplies, may be perceived more clearly when it is realized that there is often more than one edition of a work—there are three editions, at least, of the writings of Jefferson. If a footnote merely mentioned a letter of Jefferson to Adams under a certain date, without referring to the edition in which the version used is printed, the reader would experience considerable difficulty in finding the letter. It might not be included at all in the edition first examined; or if found there, might not be in the form used by the person citing it. If not, it cannot be assumed that the text reads exactly like the one used by him. Unless the footnote specifies the edition, the critical reader cannot without great difficulty determine positively what text of a document has been used.[22]

---

[22] Editors of former days sometimes took liberties with the text of documents. Jared Sparks, for instance, corrected Washington's spelling and grammar in editing his works, so that the same documents often read somewhat differently in the editions of Washington's works edited by him and by Worthington C. Ford.

The data needed for each entry in the bibliography are presumed to have been gathered during the early stages of work.[23] It has already been said that some of the data needed for books are not required for the part of the bibliography which lists periodical literature. This is because the publishers and places of publication of current journals are supposed to be generally known, or at least to be easily ascertainable; and also because each article is in a sense a separate work in itself. A bibliography accordingly should list each article separately, under the author's name, with an indication of the issue in which it is printed. To enter in the bibliography, in lieu of separate article entries, such a description of *The Century Magazine*, for example, as is given of a book, would be to conceal effectually the authorities really used, so far as they are contained in the issues of that journal. Only by thumbing through footnotes, in such a case, could the reader ascertain the authors and titles of the articles and the issues in which they are to be found. One main purpose of the bibliography is to obviate the necessity of such labor. The bibliography entry for an article practically duplicates the footnote giving the first citation of it, both in form and substance; but it is not easy to avoid the duplication in material of this class.

The reasoning which leads to the listing of articles separately is not followed so far as to lead to separate listing of documents in a collection, such as Farrand's *Records of the Federal Convention*. The proper place for specifying particular documents is the footnotes.

Bibliographical entries of essays in annuals, university studies, composite books, and similar volumes resemble book entries in some ways and article entries in others. Titles are italicized or quoted according to principles which have been explained,[24] and volume citations are required (page citations also, where the study does not fill the volume), as for periodical articles. In addition, since such volumes have definite places and dates of publication which are not so likely to be known as those of journals, they must be given as in book entries.

[23] See pages 11, 12.   [24] See pages 17, 18, 124.

Volumes forming part of series are handled in different ways. In both footnote and bibliography the volume cited should be described in its relation to the series.[25] If the volumes of the series are organic parts of the whole, as in *The American Nation*, the bibliography should contain in addition an entry describing the series.[26] If, on the other hand, it is an independent study published in series like the *Harvard Historical Studies*, there need be no series entry in the bibliography, but the publisher and place and date of publication of the individual volume should be given, in connection with the volume entry.[27]

Unlike periodical articles, newspaper items are not listed separately in the bibliography, but are treated like individual items in a collection of documents. That is, the newspaper file is described, either *in toto* or for the years for which it proved useful. Often the division of the bibliography devoted to newspapers merely lists them by name with any necessary indications of the town or state where published. The same rule holds for speeches and other matter in the records of the proceedings of Congress; that is, the separate items are not listed, but the works as a whole are described in the bibliography.

The proper forms to be used in the bibliography for government publications is sometimes a perplexing question. There can hardly be said to be a generally accepted plan. The order of entry in the library catalogue may suggest a feasible arrangement; that is, the separate items may be entered under the department, bureau, or division which issues them. When the publication bears the name of an author, editor, compiler, commission, or committee, such name gives a basis for alphabetical arrangement within the special group of items. If the publication bears a document number, that is often included in the bibliography; but it is usually omitted in the case of much-used compilations; in these there are often Plain Title editions, apart from the documentary series.

[25] For form for the footnote see page 123.
[26] See Bibliography, division headed General Histories.
[27] For illustrations of this and other usage see Bibliography.

Within each division of the bibliography the entries should be arranged alphabetically according to author, editor, or compiler. It is sometimes a puzzle to know whether the writings of a public man should be entered under his own name or that of the editor of the compilation. Should Jefferson's *Writings*, for instance, be placed under J or F (Worthington C. Ford being the editor)? One finds both forms used. It is perhaps wise in such cases to ask where a reader is most likely to look for the entry and place it there. Since the name of the editor is less likely to be known than that of the person whose writings are in question, the name of the latter should probably determine the position of the entry in most cases.

If the same author is listed more than once in the same division of the bibliography, the initial of the first significant word in the titles of his works determines the alphabetical precedence.

No very helpful suggestions can be given for arranging manuscript entries. They are best designated according to the manner in which they are stored or arranged in the depository which holds them. If one has occasion to use such collections, the local system of designations must be studied and followed. This system may be described in some publication, or it may be illustrated in the bibliography of some monograph which has been based on the collection.

4. THE FINAL REVISION

a. *Parts of a Finished Monograph*

A completed monograph should include the following parts, in the order given: (1) Title Page; (2) Preface; (3) Table of Contents; (4) Introduction; (5) Main Text, in chapters or numbered subdivisions; (6) Bibliography; and to these are often added Dedication, Appendix, and Index.

The discussion of the making of a preliminary draft has centered around items (3), (5), and (6). In the process of drafting, the working outline has developed into a Table of Contents, the Main Text, including the footnotes, has been given rough form, and the Bibliography has been classified and perhaps annotated. Before the final revision is begun, Parts (1), (2), and (4) should be added, and possibly a Dedication and Appendix. If the monograph is to have an Index, it must be supplied last of all.

If the study is designed for submission to a graduate school to meet a part of the requirements for an advanced degree, title page and general make-up must conform to specifications, which may vary somewhat from school to school. They are obtainable on request.

A Dedication is in doubtful taste; if used at all it should be modestly phrased, and not expose the author to the suspicion of vanity or self-seeking. Especially should it avoid any possibility of causing embarrassment to the person to whom it is addressed. For this reason initials of the dedicatee are usually preferable to the full name. The dedication is a matter of personal relationships, which do not much concern the public.

The function of the Preface is to enable the author to explain the purpose of the book, and if necessary, to justify the writing of it. In olden times it was called the Author's Apology. If acknowledgments are due to anyone for real aid in the preparation of the study, the preface is the proper place for making them.

The Table of Contents exhibits the location in the book of the parts of which it is composed, and especially of the divisions of the text. The main divisions may be called chapters, or, as in this manual, may be designated merely by numbered headings. Following this part of the Table there should be a list of the maps, diagrams, charts, or illustrations. Opposite each part, division, subdivision, map, etc., near the right-hand margin of the page, should be placed the number of the page on which the item, or its beginning, is to be found. The List of Maps, Charts, or Illustrations, should be the last item in the Table, following the Index.

The Introduction should define the objectives of the author, give a summary view of the scope of the work, indicate any special methods employed or bodies of material exploited, point out the place of the study in the literature of the subject, and state briefly or at least foreshadow any significant conclusions which have been reached.

Appendices are used for long quotations, documentary material, statistical tables, and other matter to which the reader should have access, but which would overload the text or make footnotes too cumbrous. Essential tables should not be relegated to an appendix, but only those of collateral significance which can be discussed just as well in that location as if they were in the text. A brief extract from a document may be sufficient to quote in the text, but there are many cases where it may be desirable to have the complete document available for the reader without the trouble of seeking it out in a library. Each item in an appendix may be called a separate appendix, and designated by a number or otherwise; or related items may be grouped in several appendices appropriately distinguished by numbers or letters.

The Index may be dispensed with in a brief treatise, if the Table of Contents is sufficiently analytical to make it an adequate guide. But no elaborate work can be easily consulted unless it is equipped with a good index. An index may be prepared by going through the manuscript and entering each name and subject on a separate slip as mention of it is found in the text, adding page numbers each time the item is encountered. Book pages can be substituted for these manuscript pages when page proof is received from the printer.

b. *Punctuation*

Judging from what one observes, most untrained writers use marks of punctuation unconsciously. Certainly there is seldom evidence of familiarity with any system of rules, or of thoughtful use. Periods at the end of sentences, a few commas dropped at random, mostly in the wrong places, with promiscuous dashes, seem to represent the total resources of this kind at the command of the average college graduate. If spelling is a lost art, punctuation as an art, for many persons, never existed.

A treatise on punctuation cannot be attempted here, but it is necessary to insist upon the importance of attention to this phase of the technique of writing. The few comments made here are offered in the hope of leading the student to pursue the subject for himself.[28]

The tendency in recent years is to minimize the use of punctuation marks, dispensing with them where they do not actually serve to make statements clearer than they would be without them. But to accomplish this they must be used thoughtfully and with discretion. That punctuation plays a significant part in determining meaning is the basic fact. The lack of punctuation in medieval manuscripts was at the root of the problem of the correct reading of the passage in Seneca's letter, discussed in an earlier section.[29] A recent writer, telling the story of Benedict Arnold, by the inadvertent insertion of a comma, changed the meaning of his statement in a startling way. Intending to write "Washington, too just to ignore his merit, made him commander in Philadelphia," he actually wrote "Washington, too, just to ignore his merit, made him commander in Philadelphia"!

The Constitution of the United States might have become the basis of a quite different type of government if an erroneous use of a semicolon had not been discovered before its final adoption. The Convention voted favorably on a provision reading:

> The Legislature shall have the power to lay and collect taxes, duties, imposts and excises, to pay the debts and provide for the common defence and general welfare of the United States.

When the Committee on Style reported the final draft, the comma after the word *excises* had been replaced by a semicolon. This made the power to promote the general welfare independent of the taxation clause—a reading which accorded with the desires of some members of the Committee, notably Gouverneur Morris, who made the draft. Through the vigilance

[28] A comprehensive yet concise discussion of punctuation will be found in Spahr and Swenson, *op. cit.*, 304–314.

[29] See pages 73, 74.

of Roger Sherman, it seems, the original punctuation was restored before the Constitution was engrossed.[30]

In punctuation as in other matters, the attempt has been made in this manual to follow correct usage so that it may be taken as a model. In lieu of a set of rules, which may be found elsewhere, stress is again laid upon the importance of *thinking* about each phase of technique until the underlying reasons are discerned—of directing the *attention* to details so that they will not be unconsciously neglected—of *deliberately* studying proper procedures until they become habitual.

A few examples may enforce the value of this general attitude. Where the structure of a sentence requires a *pair* of commas to inclose a clause or phrase, the second one is often thoughtlessly omitted. If one writes "Smith, the president of the organization, was absent," it is clear that Smith is the president. A complete statement would remain if the words set off by commas were omitted. But if the second comma were omitted, these words would become an inseparable part of the sentence, which would then apparently mean that *Smith* was a term of address, and that all that follows was by way of information imparted to him.

The use of punctuation in connection with parentheses is a stumbling block to many persons, yet one simple rule should dispel all difficulties. It is that the use of parentheses should leave the punctuation of the sentence just as it would stand if the parenthetical matter were not there. It should be added that if there is any mark of punctuation at the point where the parenthetical expression is inserted, this mark should follow the second parenthesis mark. Numerous examples of this usage will be found in the footnotes in this manual.

c. *The Literary Finish*

If one type of inexperienced writer stalls after composing a few sentences, wasting time in attempts to polish them to literary

[30] Max Farrand, *The Framing of the Constitution of the United States*, 177–179, 182. The charge against John Quincy Adams, mentioned on page 70, was that he had made a similar change in punctuation.

perfection, another type is too easily satisfied. This type, which is far more common than the other, is prone to regard as a completed product what should be looked upon as merely a preliminary draft. Between these two extremes lies the happy mean to which the vast majority of intelligent persons may be brought by proper training.

It is sometimes said that poets are born, not made. The saying is probably just as true of other good writers as it is of poets. People undoubtedly differ in natural gifts; but it is nearer the truth to say that good writing is the product of a combination in which talent is one-tenth and intelligent observation of good models and persistent practice are the other nine-tenths.

In a preliminary draft, any form of words which conveys the writer's meaning reasonably well is all that need be sought. But instead of considering such a draft as final, one of the last acts of the author should be to scrutinize the whole with the sole object of improving the literary form. The attention, especially in the case of an inexperienced writer, cannot well be concentrated on both matter and form at the same time; hence it is well to make the correction of style a separate and final process. Every word, phrase, sentence, paragraph, and division, as well as the organization of the whole monograph, should be examined for this purpose.

In this revision the writer must, of course, be on the lookout for misspelled words, erroneous punctuation, bad grammar, and violations of the rules of rhetoric. He should recall that infinitives should not be split, that "a preposition should not be used to end a sentence with," and that there are many other rules which he memorized as a schoolboy and forthwith forgot. All that he knows of formal rhetoric should now find its application.

The writer who habitually examines his work in this way is often surprised at the faults which he discovers. Correction follows as a matter of course. There are some kinds of errors, however, which escape detection so easily that it is advisable to have a competent friend go over the manuscript. Two pairs of eyes are better than one in catching slips where the meaning is clear but the grammatical construction faulty. If one writes: "After encountering a few such references, the necessity will occur to the investigator of obtaining full information," one may read the sentence several times without sensing its defects. Such errors slip into the work even of experienced writers, and often go to print for want of adequate revision of copy by a second person as well as the author. Clearly what the writer of the foregoing sentence intended to say was this: "After encountering a few such references, the investigator will perceive the necessity of obtaining full information."

But the secret of good writing lies far deeper than the careful observance of the rules of formal grammar and rhetoric. *Unconscious inattention* is the cause of much mediocre work; the chief cause of faults in writing is the *lack of the habit of looking for them*. The aspiring author must learn to observe, think, and experiment for himself.

It is a rule of some translators never to set down the English rendering of a foreign term until a half-dozen synonyms have been rehearsed mentally, in order that the words finally chosen may be those which will express the shade of meaning with the nicest accuracy. The rule would be a wise one to apply in original composition. Nothing is more essential to good writing than a rich and varied vocabulary, joined with a sensitive feeling for the right words in a given context. It is good practice to experiment with words, and also to make conscious efforts to place words and phrases in the best order or position in sentences. Sentences in a paragraph should lead to a thought climax, and each paragraph should have a unity of its own. Likewise paragraphs should be arranged in such sequence that they will lead to a climax on a higher level. By careful study of the unities, from that of the word and sentence to that of the entire monograph, and by careful arrangement of the parts so that the subordinate unities will stand in proper relations with the larger ones and the total work, an effective appeal to the reader is more likely to be made.

Many persons who are swept along by the flow of language of a master of style are conscious of its superiority without being able to detect the secret of its charm and power. They may think of it as a natural gift, when the true explanation lies in the simple habit of thoughtfully trying again and again, recasting forms of expression until they satisfy. William James confessed that every page of his *Psychology*, an epoch-making book in its day, was rewritten on the average at least six times! By such practice, far more than by any rule of thumb application of rules of rhetoric, does a writer learn how to produce the effects he desires and eventually become a facile and versatile user of the pen.

In this connection it may be repeated once more that rules are not sacred precepts like the moral law. Style is a matter of taste, and "nothing succeeds like success." Geniuses can afford to ignore rules; their powers transcend conventions; they set the new patterns which lead the rest of mankind on. Yet new fashions do not become established until they have survived severe tests. Old ways have endured because of just such survival. One essays the rôle of genius at one's own risk; ten to one, if he does, he only proves to be a consummate egotist. For ordinary persons the maxim Safety First prescribes conformity to practices which time has approved.

The point of this homily is obvious. Young writers should study the best models and follow them until their genius, if they have it, bursts confining bounds to find needed expression. Unfortunately, it is easier to follow poor models than good. Young persons are fascinated by the smartness and novelty of feature writers in newspapers and magazines. Such writing is not often frank in confessing its own weaknesses; hence the following example is doubly valuable because it illustrates one of the styles of writing in favor for the moment, and at the same time naïvely betrays the underlying reason for the style:

> Perhaps you may not like it . . . but when thoughts come hard . . . and subjects are not many . . . this is an easy way to write . . . lazy man's way of scrivening. . . .

Clarity, directness, conciseness, are safe qualities to aim at in historical writing. More than any others, these qualities catch the interest and hold the attention of readers. Innumerable tricks aid in capturing and reducing them to servitude. A careful choice of words, a correct placing of them in sentences, a merciless excision of those not needed, especially superfluous adjectives, a careful sequence in the development of ideas, a breaking of long sentences into two or more, avoidance of useless repetition—these are hints at only a few of these devices.

Clarity is in part a matter of knowing how to marshal words so that the idea to be emphasized may be thrown into relief. An unskillful assemblage of phrases may drop the idea which needs prominence to the level of the secondary, whereas an inverted phrase, or a choice of suitable introductory words in a sentence would give the desirable emphasis. If one wishes to say (1) that the *Cumulative Index* was consolidated with the *Readers' Guide*, and (2) that the independent issues are still useful, one should decide whether these statements are of equal importance. If one is secondary, a form of expression should be chosen which will subordinate it and emphasize the other. The emphasis is not precisely the same in these two ways of combining the two statements:

> The Cumulative Index is still useful because it covered some magazines which Poole did not index, but it was consolidated with the Readers' Guide in 1903.

> The Cumulative Index was consolidated with the Readers' Guide in 1903, but it is still useful because it covered . . . etc.

A statement may be drafted which contains no error, and yet on second thought it may be seen that the same things can be said more pointedly, elegantly, or forcefully. Most beginners would regard the first form of the following passage as good enough, yet it would probably be agreed that the second form is an improvement:

> While these processes are logically distinct, they are often, as a matter of fact, carried on simultaneously. Nevertheless they demand separate discussion, since each has its own technique.

These processes are, as a matter of fact, often carried on simultaneously; but they require separate discussion, since they are logically distinct and each has its own technique.

It might be difficult for an unpracticed reader to analyze these passages and explain the superiority of the second even if he felt it. One who is accustomed to careful analysis would perceive at once that the stress differs in the two forms, the second throwing into greater relief the simultaneity of the processes. Moreover, the sequence of ideas in the first is poor; the reasons why the processes require separate discussion are not well coördinated.

It is impossible to discuss exhaustively here the devices which conduce to the formation of a good style. It is much more important for the reader to realize that he must study the effects produced by phrasing thoughts in various ways, through experiments of his own, and that he must be alert to observe what the qualities are which make writers "good."

It is, however, to be noted that there is a difference between the qualities which make good historical writing and those which are desirable in so-called "polite literature." The writer of history must not forget that there is a possibility of obscuring his meaning, or the truth itself, by indulgence in figures of speech or literary effects. The fact that such habits on the part of others have caused him trouble in getting at the truth in their statements should warn him against marring his own work in similar ways. The poet and novelist have much greater license, in these respects, than the historian, whose repertory of literary artifices is restricted by the inherent nature of his subject-matter.[31]

It does not follow that the historian is condemned to a bald, plain, unattractive style. The mere use of alternative terms, to avoid constant repetition of the same words and phrases, is a simple device, but it will go far to prevent a discussion from becoming wearisome. Moreover, there is more than one way of saying a thing without sacrifice of accuracy or truthfulness. One

[31] *Cf.* pages 94–96.

may describe the Boston "Tea Party" by narrating that "about fifty men disguised as Indians went aboard the ships at the wharf and emptied 342 chests of tea into the water"; or one may say that "the radicals boarded the ships disguised as Indians, and next morning tea lay strewn like sea weed along Dorchester beach."

These two statements, to be sure, do not relate precisely the same facts, for the first says expressly that the boarding party emptied the tea into the water and gives the exact number of chestsful.   The second, however, leaves no doubt as to the essential happening, even though the number of chests (a detail of no use to the reader even if he could remember it) is not told. The first account is a prosy narrative weighted with ineffectual details.   The second is comparatively interesting; it is just as informing, and it challenges the imagination.

Another legitimate method of enlivening style, if one is not adept at coining original phrases, is to use a moderate spice of racy quotations. Conditions in the Illinois settlements on the eve of George Rogers Clark's campaign may be described in prosaic terms setting forth England's inability to maintain an adequate garrison on that remote frontier.   If a catchy yet truthful phrase can be thrown into the midst of such a narrative, it may stimulate the flagging interest of the reader.   Thus of Kaskaskia it might be said: "Here, as at most of the posts, only the 'flicker of a red flag' showed that the land was British."

For the sake of relieving the monotony of statement after statement of bare facts, it is permissible now and then, when the topic permits, to indulge in a bit of color. Details of peace terms and territorial transfers following the French and Indian War may justifiably lead up to a description of the significance of the British victory in which the writer spreads his wings somewhat more than usual:

> With their defeat the French Bourbons made their exit from the North American mainland and the curtain fell upon the dramatic and colorful history of New France; the turbid waters of the Mississippi marked the eastward limits of the dominions

of decadent Spain, and half a continent spread its invitation before the restless feet of the sturdy race whose multiplying paths led westward from the margin of the Atlantic.

Too many literary flourishes, however, may make the style florid, stilted, or affected. In that case it is likely to become even more boresome to an intelligent reader than a tale without adornment. And above all, embellishment must never become a first aim, or be allowed to hide or distort the truth.

BIBLIOGRAPHY

The purpose of this Bibliography is twofold: (1) to give a helpful list of works relating to historical research; and (2) to illustrate the forms in which bibliographical entries should be drawn up. It is therefore divided into two parts.

PART I. WORKS RELATING TO HISTORICAL RESEARCH

1. *Books on Historical Method*

Almack, John C., *Research and Thesis Writing: A Textbook on the Principles and Techniques of Thesis Construction for the Use of Graduate Students in Universities and Colleges.* Houghton Mifflin Company, Boston [c1930].

Bernheim, Ernst, *Lehrbuch der Historischen Methode und der Geschichtsphilosophie. . . .* 6th edn. Duncker & Humblot, Leipzig, 1908.

Chicago University Press, *A Manual of Style, Containing Typographical Rules Governing the Publications of the University of Chicago. . . .* University of Chicago Press, Chicago, 1927.

Dow, Earle W., *Principles of a Note-System.* The Century Co., New York, 1924.

Fling, Fred Morrow, *The Writing of History: An Introduction to Historical Method.* Yale University Press, New Haven, 1920.

Gee, Wilson, ed., *Research in the Social Sciences: Its Fundamental Methods and Objectives.* The Macmillan Company, New York, 1929.

Hutchins, Margaret, Alice Sarah Johnson, and Margaret Stuart Williams, *Guide to the Use of Libraries: A Manual for College and University Students.* 4th edn. The H. W. Wilson Company, New York, 1929.

Johnson, Allen, *The Historian and Historical Evidence.* Charles Scribner's Sons, New York, 1926.

Jusserand, Jean Jules, Wilbur Cortez Abbott, Charles W. Colby, and John Spencer Bassett, *The Writing of History.* Charles Scribner's Sons, New York [c1926].

Langlois, Charles V., and Charles Seignobos, *Introduction to the Study of History. Translated by G. G. Berry.* Henry Holt and Company, New York, 1912.

Nevins, Allan, *Masters' Essays in History: A Manual of Instructions and Suggestions.* Columbia University Press, New York, 1930.

Odum, H. W., and Kath. Jocher, *An Introduction to Social Research.* Henry Holt and Company, New York, 1929.

Reeder, Ward G., *How to Write a Thesis.* Public School Publishing Company, Bloomington, Ill. [c1925].

Rice, Stuart A., ed., *Methods in Social Science: A Case Book. Compiled under the Direction of the Committee on Scientific Method in the Social Sciences of the Social Science Research Council.* University of Chicago Press, Chicago [c1931].

Schluter, W. C., *How to Do Research Work: A Manual of Research Procedure Presenting a Simple Explanation of the Principles Underlying Research Methods.* Prentice-Hall, Inc., New York, 1926.

Spahr, Walter Earl, and Rinehart John Swenson, *Methods and Status of Scientific Research; with Particular Application to the Social Sciences.* Harper & Brothers, New York, 1930.

Thornton, Harrison John, and John William Ashton, *Dissertations in History and English.* University of Iowa *Studies*, 1 series, No. 183. University of Iowa, Iowa City, 1930.

Vincent, John Martin, *Historical Research: An Outline of Theory and Practice.* Henry Holt and Company, New York, 1911.

2. *General Guides to Reference Works*

Mudge, Isadore G., *et al.*, comp., *Guide to Reference Books.* 6th edn. American Library Association, Chicago, 1936.

Mudge, Isadore G., Doris M. Reed, and Constance M. Winchell, *Reference Books of 1929. An Informal Supplement to Guide to Reference Books.* American Library Association, Chicago, 1930.

3. *General Catalogues of Books*

American Catalogue of Books, 1876–1910. 9 vols. Publishers' Weekly, New York, 1881–1911.

Annual American Catalogue, 1886–1910. Publishers' Weekly, New York, 1887–1911.

Cumulative Book Index, 1898–   . The H. W. Wilson Company, New York, 1898–   .

Evans, Charles, *American Bibliography.* 10 vols. (1930). Blakely Press, Chicago, 1903–1929.

Kelly, James, *American Catalogue of Books Published in the United States from January, 1861, to January, 1871.* 2 vols. Wiley, New York, 1866–1871.

Publishers' Weekly, January, 1872–   . Publishers' Weekly, New York, 1872–   .

Roorbach, Orville Augustus, *Bibliotheca Americana, 1820–1861*. 4 vols. Roorbach, New York, 1852–1861.

Sabin, Joseph, *Dictionary of Books Relating to America, from Its Discovery to the Present Time*. 21 vols. (1930). J. Sabin, New York, 1868–1929.

United States Catalogue, 1900– . Edited by Marion E. Potter *et al.* The H. W. Wilson Company, New York, 1900– .

4. *Guides to Appraisal of Books*

Allison, William Henry, Sidney Bradshaw Fay, *et al.*, eds., *A Guide to Historical Literature*. The Macmillan Company, New York, 1931.

Book Review Digest, 1905– . The H. W. Wilson Company, New York, 1905– .

Larned, Josephus Nelson, ed., *The Literature of American History*. Houghton Mifflin Company, Boston, 1902.

—*Supplement* for 1900 and 1901, ed. by P. P. Wells (American Library Association *Annotated Lists*). American Library Association Publishing Board, Boston, 1902.

—*Supplements* for 1902 and 1903, ed. by P. P. Wells (*Annotated Titles of Books on English and American History*). American Library Association Publishing Board, Boston, 1903–1904.

—*Supplement* for 1904. American Library Association Publishing Board, Boston, 1905.

5. *Indexes of Periodical Literature*

a. GENERAL

American Library Annual, 1911– . Publishers' Weekly, New York, 1912– .

Annual Library Index, 1905–1910. 6 vols. Publishers' Weekly, New York, 1906–1911.

Annual Literary Index, 1892–1904. 13 vols. Publishers' Weekly, New York, 1893–1905.

Annual Magazine Subject-Index, 1908– . Faxon, Boston, 1909– .

Cumulative Index to a Selected List of Periodicals, 1896–1903. 8 vols. Cumulative Index Company, Cleveland, 1897–1903.

Gregory, Winifred, comp., *Union List of Serials in Libraries of the United States and Canada*. H. W. Wilson Company, New York, 1927.

International Index to Periodicals, 1920– . The H. W. Wilson Company, New York, 1921– .

Magazine Subject-Index. Boston Book Company, Boston, 1908.

Poole's Index to Periodical Literature, 1802–1881. Rev. edn. 2 vols. Houghton Mifflin Company, Boston, 1891.

—*Supplements*, January, 1882–January, 1907. 5 vols. Houghton Mifflin Company, Boston, 1887–1908.

—*Abridgment.* Houghton Mifflin Company, Boston, 1901.

—*Supplement to Abridgment*, 1900–1904. Houghton Mifflin Company, Boston, 1905.

Readers' Guide to Periodical Literature, 1900– . The H. W. Wilson Company, New York, 1900– .

—*Supplement*, 1907–1919. 2 vols. The H. W. Wilson Company, New York, 1916–1920.

Social Science Abstracts, 1929– . Menasha, Wis., 1929– .

b. LAW PERIODICALS

Index to Legal Periodicals, 1908– (published in conjunction with the *Law Library Journal*). The H. W. Wilson Company, New York, 1909– .

Jones, Leonard Augustus, *Index to Legal Periodical Literature.* 3 vols. Boston Book Company, Boston, 1888–1919.

C. NEWSPAPER INDEXES AND CHECKLISTS

Brigham, Clarence S., *Bibliography of American Newspapers, 1690–1820*, in American Antiquarian Society *Proceedings*, n. s., XXIII, Part 2, 247–402, and succeeding volumes.

New York Daily Tribune Index, 1875–1906. 31 vols. Tribune Association, New York, 1876–1907.

New York Times Index. New York Times, New York, 1913– .

Slauson, A. B., comp., *Check-List of American Newspapers in the Library of Congress. . . .* Government Printing Office, Washington, 1901.

6. *Bibliographies of Bibliographies*

Channing, Edward, Albert Bushnell Hart, and Frederick Jackson Turner, *Guide to the Study and Reading of American History.* Rev. edn. Ginn and Company, Boston, 1912.

Coulter, Edith M., *Guide to Historical Bibliographies. A Critical and Systematic Bibliography for Advanced Students.* University of California Press, Berkeley, 1927. Rev. edn., 1935.

Hart, Albert Bushnell, ed., *The American Nation: A History.* 28 vols. Harper & Brothers, New York, 1904–1918.

Matteson, David Maydole, *General Index to Papers and Annual Reports of the American Historical Association, 1884–1914.* (American Historical Association *Annual Report* for 1914, II.) Government Printing Office, Washington, 1918.

Schlesinger, Arthur M., and Dixon Ryan Fox, eds., *A History of American Life.* 6 vols. (1930). The Macmillan Company, New York, 1927– .

Winsor, Justin, ed., *Narrative and Critical History of America.* 8 vols. Houghton Mifflin Company, Boston, 1884–1889.

7. *Bibliographies of American History*

Griffin, Appleton Prentiss Clark, comp., *Bibliography of American Historical Societies.* (American Historical Association *Annual Report* for 1905, II.) Government Printing Office, Washington, 1907.

Writings on American History, 1902, . . . by E. C. Richardson and A. E. Morse. Library Book Store, Princeton, N. J., 1904.

—1903, by A. C. McLaughlin, *et al.* Carnegie Institution, Washington, 1905.

—1906– , by Grace Gardner Griffin. 1906–1908, The Macmillan Company, New York, 1908–1910. 1909–1911, Government Printing Office, Washington, 1911–1913. 1912–1917, Yale University Press, New Haven, 1914–1919. 1918– , Government Printing Office, Washington, 1921– .

8. *Guides and Indexes for Government Publications*

Ames, John G., *Comprehensive Index to the Publications of the United States Government, 1881–1893.* 2 vols. Government Printing Office, Washington, 1905.

Clarke, Edith E., *Guide to the Use of United States Government Documents.* The Boston Book Company, Boston, 1918.

Church, Alonzo Webster, and Henry H. Smith, *Tables Showing the Contents of the Several Volumes Comprising the Annals of Congress, Congressional Debates, Congressional Globe, Congressional Record, Statutes at Large, U. S. Supreme Court Reports, Arranged by Years and Congresses.* Government Printing Office, Washington [1892].

Everhart, Elfrida. *A Handbook of United States Public Documents.* The H. W. Wilson Company, Minneapolis, 1910.

Hasse, Adelaide R., *Index to United States Documents Relating to Foreign Affairs, 1828–1861.* (Carnegie Institution *Publication No. 185.*) Carnegie Institution, Washington, 1914.

Poore, Benjamin Perley, *Descriptive Catalogue of the Government Publications of the United States, 1774–1881.* Government Printing Office, Washington, 1885.

United States Superintendent of Documents, *Catalogue of the Public Documents of Congress and of All Departments of the Government, 1893–* . Government Printing Office, Washington, 1896– .

United States Superintendent of Documents, *Checklist of United States Public Documents, 1789–1909.* 3d edn., rev. and enlarged. Government Printing Office, Washington, 1911.

United States Superintendent of Documents, *Monthly Catalogue of United States Public Documents,* 1895–   . Government Printing Office, Washington, 1895–   .

United States Superintendent of Documents, *Tables of and Annotated Index to the Congressional Series of United States Public Documents.* Government Printing Office, Washington, 1902.

9. *Guides to Archives and Manuscripts*

Garrison, C. W., "Survey of the Manuscript Collections in the Library of Congress." Volume I of the American Historical Association *Annual Report* for 1930.

Jameson, J. F., Chairman, Historical Manuscripts Commission of the American Historical Association, "Items Respecting Historical Manuscripts," including public and private collections. Third annual report of the Commission, in American Historical Association *Annual Report* for 1898, 565–708.

Matteson, David M., comp., *List of Manuscripts Concerning American History Preserved in European Libraries and Noted in Their Published Catalogues and Similar Printed Lists.* Carnegie Institution, Washington, 1925.

United States, Library of Congress, *Publications Issued . . . since 1897.* Government Printing Office, Washington, 1929.

United States, Library of Congress, Division of Manuscripts, *Checklist of Collections of Personal Papers in Historical Societies, University and Public Libraries, and Other Learned Institutions in the United States.* Government Printing Office, Washington, 1918.

United States, Library of Congress, Division of Manuscripts, *Handbook of Manuscripts in the Library of Congress.* Government Printing Office, Washington, 1918.

Van Tyne, Claude Halstead, and Walter G. Leland, comps., *Guide to the Archives of the Government of the United States in Washington.* Rev. edn. Carnegie Institution, Washington, 1907.

(For full list of Guides to Archives published by the Carnegie Institution, see Mudge, *Guide to Reference Books,* index.)

10. *Bibliographies for Local History**

a. RELATING TO ALL STATES

Bowker, Richard R., *State Publications.* 4 vols. Publishers' Weekly, New York, 1899–1909.

* This list is intended to be representative; it is far from exhaustive and complete.

Bradford, Thomas L., *Bibliographer's Manual of American History, Ed. and Revised by S. V. Henkels*. 5 vols. Henkels, Philadelphia, 1907–1910.

Carnegie Institution, *Handbook of Learned Societies and Institutions: American*. Carnegie Institution, Washington, 1908.

Childs, James B., *An Account of Government Document Bibliography in the United States and Elsewhere*. Government Printing Office, Washington, 1927.

Hasse, Adelaide R., *Index of Economic Material in Documents of the States of the United States*. 13 vols. Carnegie Institution, Washington, 1907–1922.

United States, Library of Congress, Division of Documents, *Monthly Check List of State Publications*, 1909– . Government Printing Office, Washington, 1910– .

b. REGIONAL

Original States

Andrews, Charles M., "Lists of Reports and Representations of Plantation Councils . . . in the Public Record Office." American Historical Association *Annual Report* for 1913, I, 319–496.

Greene, Evarts B., and R. B. Morris, comps., *Guide to the Principal Sources for Early American History (1600–1800) in the City of New York*. Columbia University Press, New York, 1929.

Hasse, Adelaide R., "Materials for a Bibliography of the Public Archives of the Thirteen Original States, Covering the Colonial Period and the State Period to 1789." American Historical Association *Annual Report* for 1906, II, 239–561.

Jameson, J. Franklin, "Colonial Assemblies and their Legislative Journals." American Historical Association *Annual Report* for 1897, 405–453.

South

Beer, William, "Bibliographical Notes on Materials Relating to the History of the Gulf States." *Gulf States Historical Magazine*, I, 419–422 (May, 1903).

Boyd, William Kenneth, and Robert Preston Brooks, comps., *A Selected Bibliography and Syllabus of the History of the South, 1584–1876*. The McGregor Company, Athens, Ga., 1918.

Freeman, Douglas Southall, *A Calendar of Confederate Papers, with a Bibliography of Some Confederate Publications*. Confederate Museum, Richmond, Va., 1908.

Morrison, Hugh A., "A Bibliography of the Official Publications of the Confederate States of America." Bibliographical Society of America *Proceedings and Papers*, III, 92–132 (1909).

Virginia State Library, "A List of the Official Publications of the Confederate States Government in the Virginia State Library, and the Library of the Confederate Memorial Literary Society." Virginia State Library *Bulletin*, IV, No. 1, 1–72 (January, 1911).

Mississippi Valley

Surrey, Nancy M., *Calendar of Manuscripts in Paris Archives and Libraries Relating to the History of the Mississippi Valley to 1803.* 2 vols. Carnegie Institution, Washington, 1926–1928.

Thwaites, Reuben G., *Descriptive List of Manuscript Collections of the Society, Together with Reports on other Collections of Manuscript Material for American History in Adjacent States.* Wisconsin Historical Society, Madison, 1906.

Pacific Coast

Chapman, C. E., *Catalogue of Materials in the Archivo General de Indias for the History of the Pacific Coast and the American Southwest.* University of California Press, Berkeley, 1919.

Judson, K. B., *Subject Index to the History of the Pacific Northwest and Alaska.* Washington State Library, Olympia, 1913.

Smith, Charles Wesley, *Pacific Northwest Americana.* 2d edn. The H. W. Wilson Company, New York, 1921.

Smith, Charles W., *A Union List of Manuscripts in Libraries of the Pacific Northwest.* University of Washington Press, Seattle, 1931.

c. ALPHABETICALLY BY STATES

Arizona

Alliot, Hector, *Bibliography of Arizona: Being the Record of Literature Collected by Dr. J. A. Munk, and Donated by Him to the Southwest Museum.* The Southwest Museum, Los Angeles, 1914.

Lutrell, Estelle, *A Bibliographical List of Books, Pamphlets and Articles on Arizona in the University of Arizona Library.* University of Arizona *Record*, ser. VI, No. 10 (1913).

Arkansas

Herndon, Dallas T., Secy. Arkansas History Commission, "Bibliography of Historical and Literary Writings of Arkansans." History Commission *Bulletin of Information No. 4.* Little Rock, 1912.

Reynolds, John Hugh, "An Account of Books, Records, and Manuscripts [concerning Arkansas] in Public Repositories within the State." Arkansas Historical Association *Publications*, I, 110–185.

Reynolds, John Hugh, "An Account of Books, Manuscripts, Documents, and Papers [concerning Arkansas] in Private Hands." Arkansas Historical Association *Publications*, I, 230–273.

Reynolds, John Hugh, "An Account of Manuscripts, Papers, and Documents Concerning Arkansas in Public Repositories beyond the State." Arkansas Historical Association *Publications*, I, 43–109.

California

Baker, C. C., "A List of Newspapers in the Los Angeles City Library." Southern California Historical Society *Publications*, X, Parts 1 and 2, 80–85.

Bancroft, Hubert Howe, "Authorities Consulted on the History of California." In *Works*, XVIII, xxv–lxxxviii.

Cowan, Robert Ernest, *A Bibliography of the History of California and the Pacific West, 1510–1906*. Book Club of California, San Francisco, 1914.

Huntington Library, *Bulletin* No. 1, containing a brief description of one hundred of the most important accessions. Harvard University Press, Cambridge, Mass., 1931.

Colorado

Paxson, Frederic Logan, "A Preliminary Bibliography of Colorado History." Colorado University *Studies*, III, No. 3, Part 1, 101–114 (1906).

Connecticut

Flagg, Charles A., *Reference List on Connecticut Local History*. University of the State of New York, Albany, 1900.

Yale University Library, "A List of Newspapers in the Yale University Library." *Yale Historical Publications, Miscellany*, II. Yale University Press, New Haven, 1916.

Georgia

Brooks, Robert Preston, "A Preliminary Bibliography of Georgia History." University of Georgia *Bulletin*, X, No. 10 A. The McGregor Company, Athens, 1910.

Wegelin, Oscar, comp., *Books Relating to the History of Georgia in the Library of Wymberley Jones De Renne, of Wormsloe, Isle of Hope, Chatham County, Georgia*. Morning News, Savannah, 1911.

Illinois

Buck, Solon Justus, *Travel and Description, 1765–1865*, . . . Illinois
State Historical Library *Collections*, IX, *Bibliographical Series* II.
Illinois State Historical Library, Springfield, 1914.

James, Edmund J., and Milo J. Loveless, *A Bibliography of Newspapers
Published in Illinois Prior to 1860.* Illinois State Historical Library
Publications, No. 1. Springfield, 1899.

Osborne, Georgia L., *A List of the Genealogical Works in the Illinois
State Historical Library.* Illinois State Historical Library, Springfield, 1914.

Indiana

Henley, Lillian E., "Bibliography of Town and City Histories in the
Indiana State Library." *Indiana Magazine of History,* VI, 91–95
(June, 1910).

Indiana Historical Society, *A Descriptive Catalogue of the Official Publications of the Territory and State of Indiana from 1800 to 1890.*
Pamphlet No. 5. Indianapolis, 1890.

Indiana State Library, "Bibliography of Indiana Local History Contained in County Histories, Atlases, and Collected Biographies."
Bulletin No. V, 3–8 (March, 1910).

Indiana State Library, "A List of Indiana Newspapers Available in the
Indiana State Library, the Indianapolis Public Library, the Library
of Indiana University, and the Library of Congress. . . ." *Bulletin
No. XI*, 1–31 (Dec., 1916).

Indiana State Library, "A Select Bibliography of Indiana Historical
Material in the Indiana State Library." *Bulletin No. X*, 2–16
(Sept., 1915).

Iowa

Brigham, Johnson, "A General Survey of the Literature of Iowa
History." *Iowa Journal of History*, I, 77–104 (Jan., 1903).

Fitzpatrick, T. J., "Bibliography of the Iowa Territorial Documents."
Iowa Journal of History, V, 234–269 (April, 1907).

Iowa Library Commission, *Checklist of the Publications of the State of
Iowa, with an Index to the Iowa Documents.* Iowa Library Commission, Des Moines, 1904.

Kansas

Connelley, William E., *A List of Kansas Newspapers. From the Newspaper Section of the State Historical Society.* State Printing Office,
Topeka, 1914.

Kansas State Historical Society, *A List of Books Indispensable to a Knowledge of Kansas History and Literature.* . . . State Printing Plant, Topeka, 1916.

Kansas State Library, "List of One Hundred Books by Kansas Authors or Authors Writing about Kansas." Twentieth Biennial *Report* of the State Librarian, 11–14. Topeka, 1916.

Maine

Williamson, Joseph, *Bibliography of Maine.* 2 vols. Portland, 1896.

Maryland

The Michael Jenkins Collection of Works on the History of Maryland. Catholic University of America, Washington, 1913.

Massachusetts

Flagg, Charles A., *A Guide to Massachusetts Local History; Being a Bibliographic Index to the Literature of the Towns, Cities, and Counties of the State, including Books, Pamphlets, Articles in Periodicals and Collected Works, Books in Preparation, Historical Manuscripts, Newspaper Clippings, etc.* Salem Press, Salem, Mass., 1907.

Michigan

Michigan State Library, *Genealogy and American Local History in the Michigan State Library.* 2d edn., revised and enlarged. Lansing, 1915.

Mississippi

Mississippi Historical Society, "An Account of Manuscripts, Papers and Documents in the Public Repositories within the State of Mississippi." Mississippi Historical Society *Publications*, V, 119–227 (1902).

Mississippi Historical Society, "An Account of Manuscripts, Papers, and Documents Pertaining to Mississippi in Public Repositories beyond the State." Mississippi Historical Society *Publications*, V, 49–117 (1902).

Owen, Thomas McAdory, "A Bibliography of Mississippi." American Historical Association *Report* for 1899, I, 633–828.

Robinson, Mary, "Mississippi Newspaper Files in the Library of the American Antiquarian Society, Worcester, Mass." (to 1868). *Gulf States Historical Magazine*, II, 50–53 (July, 1903).

Rowland, Dunbar, Lists of Documents in England, France, and Spain, 1540–1798, of value for Mississippi History. *Fifth Annual*

Report of the Director of the Mississippi Department of Archives and History. Brandon Printing Company, Nashville, Tenn., 1907.

Missouri

Missouri State Historical Society, *List of Old Newspapers in the Library of the State Historical Society of Missouri.* The Society, Columbia, 1911.

Moody, Katherine Twining, "Genealogical Material in the St. Louis Public Library." St. Louis Public Library *Monthly Bulletin*, XIII, No. 8, 223–254 (August, 1915).

Sampson, Francis Asbury, "Bibliography of Books of Travel in Missouri." *Missouri Historical Review*, VI, 64–81 (Jan., 1912).

New Jersey

Johnson, Maude E., "A Bibliography of New Jersey Bibliographies." New Jersey Historical Society *Proceedings*, 3d series, X, 61–62 (April, 1915).

New York

Buffalo Historical Society, "Rough List of Manuscripts in the Library of the Buffalo Historical Society." Buffalo Historical Society *Publications*, XIV, 421–485 (Appendix B) (1910).

Flagg, Charles A., and Judson T. Jennings, *Bibliography of New York Colonial History.* New York State Library *Bulletin, No. 56* (Feb., 1901).

Haskell, Daniel C., *Check-list of Newspapers and Official Gazettes in the New York Public Library.* New York Public Library, New York, 1915.

Hasse, Adelaide R., "Some Materials for a Bibliography of the Official Publications of the General Assembly of the Colony of New York, 1693–1775." New York Public Library *Bulletin*, VII, 51–79, 95–116, 129–151 (Feb.–April, 1903).

Jewett, Alice Louise, *Official Publications of the State of New York Relating to its History as Colony and State.* New York State Library. *Bibliography Bulletin No. 59* (1917).

Mix, David E. E., *Catalogue of Maps and Surveys in the Offices of the Secretary of State, State Engineer and Surveyor, and Comptroller, and the New York State Library.* Revised. Printed by order of the Assembly. Albany, 1859.

New York State Library, *Annotated List of the Principal Manuscripts in the New York State Library. History Bulletin No. 3* (June, 1899).

New York State Library, *Descriptive List of French Manuscripts Copied for the New York State Library from the National Archives and National Library at Paris, 1888. History Bulletin No. 5* (1902).

Severance, Frank Hayward, "Contributions towards a Bibliography
of the Niagara Region. Pamphlets and Books Printed in Buffalo
prior to 1850." Buffalo Historical Society *Publications*, VI, Appendix
(1903).

North Carolina

North Carolina State Library, *A Bibliography of North Carolina. . . .
Biennial Report . . . for . . . years ending November 30, 1918*, 23-
80. Raleigh, 1919.
Weeks, Stephen Beauregard, *A Select Bibliography of North Carolina.
List of Books for Schools, Libraries, and Amateurs.* North Carolina
Library Commission, Raleigh, 1913.
Weeks, Stephen Beauregard, *A Bibliography of the Historical Literature
of North Carolina.* Harvard University Library, *Bibliographical Con-
tributions*, ed. by Justin Winsor, *No. 48.* Library of Harvard Uni-
versity, Cambridge, 1895.

Ohio

Baldwin, Charles Candee, *Early Maps of Ohio and the West.* Western
Reserve Historical Society, Cleveland, 1875.
Hayes, R. P., *Publications of the State of Ohio, 1803-1896, together with
an Index to the Executive Documents.* The Laning Printing Company,
Norwalk, 1897.
Historical and Philosophical Society of Ohio, *A Partial List of the Books
in Its Library Relating to the State of Ohio.* The Society, Cincinnati,
1893.
Ryan, Daniel Joseph, *The Civil War Literature of Ohio; A Bibliography
with Explanatory and Historical Notes.* Burrows Brothers Company,
Cleveland, 1911.
State Supervisor of Public Printing, *Official List of Newspapers Pub-
lished in Ohio.* The F. J. Heer Printing Company, Columbus,
1916.
Stevenson, Richard Taylor, "A Preliminary Report on the Archives of
Ohio." American Historical Association *Annual Report* for 1906, II,
165-196.
Thomson, Peter G., *A Bibliography of the State of Ohio.* The Author,
Cincinnati, 1880.
Thwaites, Reuben G., *Descriptive List of Manuscript Collections. . . .*
Wisconsin Historical Society, Madison, 1906.

Rhode Island

Chapin, Howard M., *Bibliography of Rhode Island Bibliography.* Preston & Rounds, Providence, 1914.

South Carolina

Whitney, Edson L., "Bibliography of South Carolina." American Historical Association *Annual Report* for 1894, 563-586.

Texas

Texas State Library and Historical Commission, "Calendar of the Mirabeau Buonaparte Lamar Papers." State Library *Report*, 1911–1912, Part II, 7-315. Austin, 1914. "Check List of Transcripts from the Archives of Mexico." *Ibid.*, 46-64. "List of Transcripts from the British Public Records Office." *Ibid.*, appendices 2 and 3.

Virginia

Minor, Mrs. Kate Pleasants, *et al.*, "A List of Newspapers in the Virginia State Library, Confederate Museum, and Valentine Museum." Virginia State Library *Bulletin*, V, *No. 4* (Oct., 1912), 285-425.

Swem, Earl G., "A Bibliography of the Conventions and Constitutions of Virginia, including References to Essays, Letters, and Speeches in Virginia Newspapers." Virginia State Library *Bulletin*, III, *No. 4* (Oct., 1910), 355-441.

Swem, Earl G., "A Bibliography of Virginia." Part I in Virginia State Library *Bulletin*, VIII, *Nos. 2-4*, 31-767 (1915); Part II in *Bulletin*, X, *Nos. 1-4* (Jan.-Oct., 1917); Part III in *Bulletin*, XII, *Nos. 1-2* (Jan.-Apr., 1919).

Torrence, William Clayton, *A Trial Bibliography of Colonial Virginia.* In *Fifth–Sixth Annual Report* of the Library Board of the Virginia State Library. Richmond, 1908-1910.

Wisconsin

Wisconsin State Historical Society, *Annotated Catalogue of Newspaper Files in the Library of the Wisconsin State Historical Society.* 2d edn. The Society, Madison, 1911.

Wisconsin State Historical Society, *Supplementary Catalogue of Newspaper Files in the Wisconsin Historical Library, Listing the Papers Acquired . . . 1911–1917. Bulletin of Information, No. 93.* The Society, Madison, 1918.

Wisconsin State Historical Society, *Catalogue of Books on the War of the Rebellion, and Slavery, in the Library.* The Society, Madison, 1887.

Wisconsin State Historical Society, *Checklist of Publications of the Society, 1850–1913. Bulletin of Information, No. 67.* The Society, Madison [1913].

Wisconsin State Historical Society, *Descriptive List of Manuscript Collections of the Society. . . .* The Society, Madison, 1906.

PART II. WORKS MENTIONED IN THE MANUAL BUT NOT INCLUDED IN PART I

1. *Government Publications*

American State Papers, edited by Walter Lowrie *et al.* 38 vols. Gales and Seaton, Washington, 1833–1861.

Annals of the Congress of the United States, 1789–1825. Gales and Seaton, Washington, 1834–1856.

Congressional Globe, 1834–1873. Blair & Rives (*et al.*), editors and publishers. Washington, 1834–1873.

Congressional Record, 1874– . Government Printing Office, Washington, 1874– .

Donaldson, Thomas, *The Public Domain.* 47 Cong., 2 sess., *H. Misc. Doc. 45, Pt. 4.*

Ford, Worthington C., and Gaillard Hunt, eds., *Journals of the Continental Congress, 1774–1789.* 25 vols. (1774–1783). Government Printing Office, Washington, 1904–1922.

Kappler, C. J., comp., *Indian Affairs, Laws and Treaties.* 57 Cong., 1 sess., *Sen. Doc. 452.*

Register of Debates in Congress, 1825–1837. Gales and Seaton, Washington, 1825–1837.

Richardson, James Daniel, comp., *A Compilation of the Messages and Papers of the Presidents, 1789–1897.* 10 vols. Government Printing Office, Washington, 1896–1900.

The Statutes at Large of the United States . . . 1789–1873. 17 vols. Little and Brown (later Little, Brown and Company), Boston, 1845–1873.

The Statutes at Large of the United States, 1873– . Volume 18 *et seq.* Government Printing Office, Washington, 1875– .

2. *Newspapers*

Baltimore Sun.
Christian Science Monitor (Boston).
New York Times.
Public Opinion (New York).
Springfield Republican (Mass.).

3. *Biographies, Memoirs, and Writings of Public Men*

Madison, James, *Papers of James Madison, Being his Correspondence and Reports of Debates*, edited by Henry D. Gilpin. 3 vols., Washington, 1840.

Washington, George, *The Writings of George Washington*, edited by
Worthington C. Ford. 14 vols. G. P. Putnam's Sons, New York,
1889–1893.

4. *General Histories*

Hart, Albert Bushnell, ed., *The American Nation: A History*. 28 vols.
Harper & Brothers, New York, 1904–1918.
Sparks, Edwin Erle, *National Development, 1877–1885* (volume XXIII
of *The American Nation*, ed. by A. B. Hart).

5. *Special Monographs*

Bernard, George S., *Civil Service Reform versus the Spoils System*.
J. B. Alden, New York, 1885.
Civil Service Reform Association, *Bibliography of Civil Service Reform
and Related Subjects*. Published for the Women's Auxiliary to the Civil
Service Reform Association. New York, 1900.
Farrand, Max, *The Framing of the Constitution of the United States*.
Yale University Press, New Haven, 1913.
Fish, Carl Russell, *The Civil Service and the Patronage (Harvard Histor-
ical Studies*, XI). Longmans, Green and Company, New York, 1905.
Lambert, Henry, *Progress of Civil Service Reform in the United States*.
Boston, 1885.

6. *Articles and Essays in Periodicals, Annuals, and Publications of
Learned Societies*

Adams, Herbert Baxter, "Maryland's Influence upon Land Cessions"
(Johns Hopkins University *Studies in History and Political Science*,
III, No. 1). Johns Hopkins University, Baltimore, 1885.
Angle, Paul M., "The Minor Collection: A Criticism." *Atlantic
Monthly*, CXLIII, 516–525 (April, 1929).
Bassett, John Spencer, "The Regulators of North Carolina (1765–
1771)." American Historical Association *Annual Report* for 1894,
141–212.
Beale, Howard K., "Is the Printed Diary of Gideon Welles Reliable?"
American Historical Review, XXX, 547–552 (April, 1925).
Cary, Edward, "The Administration and Civil Service Reform."
International Review, VI, 227–233 (March, 1879).
Dunning, William A., "More Light on Andrew Johnson." *American
Historical Review*, XI, 574–594 (April, 1906).
Esarey, Logan, "The Organization of the Jacksonian Party in Indiana."
Mississippi Valley Historical Association *Proceedings* for 1913–1914,
220–243.

Gephart, William F., *Transportation and Industrial Development in the Middle West* (Columbia University *Studies in Economics, History, and Public Law*, XXXIV). Columbia University, New York, 1922.

Hockett, Homer C., "The Literary Motive in the Writing of History." *Mississippi Valley Historical Review*, XII, 469–482 (March, 1926).

Houston, David Franklin, *A Critical Study of Nullification in South Carolina (Harvard Historical Studies*, III). Longmans, Green and Company, New York, 1898.

Jameson, John Franklin, "Studies in the History of the Federal Convention." American Historical Association *Annual Report* for 1902, I, 89–167.

Quaife, Milo M., "A Critical Evaluation of the Sources for Western History." *Mississippi Valley Historical Review*, I, 167–184 (Sept., 1914).

Rhodes, James Ford, "Newspapers as Historical Sources." *Historical Essays*, 81–97. The Macmillan Company, New York, 1909.

7. *Miscellaneous*

Becker, Carl Lotus, "Kansas." *Essays in American History dedicated to Frederick Jackson Turner*, 85–111. Henry Holt and Company, New York, 1910.

Chandler, William E., "Chester A. Arthur" (in *The Presidents of the United States, 1789–1914,* by John Fiske, . . . and many others, edited by James Grant Wilson. 4 vols. Charles Scribner's Sons, New York, 1914), III, 195–237.

Johnson, Allen, ed., *The Dictionary of American Biography.* Charles Scribner's Sons, New York, 1928–   .

Who's Who in America. Biennial. A. N. Marquis and Company, Chicago.

INDEX

Abbreviations, use of in footnotes, 120–123; list of, 125.

Adams, James Truslow, 92.

Adams, John, on authorship of Declaration of Independence, 102

Adams, John Quincy, and Pinckney Plan, 67; charged with falsifying text of Constitution, 70; *Memoirs* of, 70 n., 81, 87, 100; on claim to Texas, 87; as diarist, 88; on Calhoun's opinion of Missouri Compromise, 100, 103; alleged bargain with Clay, 103; in House election of 1825, 105–111.

Allusions, as facts, 98–99.

American Antiquarian Society, 61.

American Catalogue of Books, 27.

American Historical Association, publications, 6; as model for forms, 16; relations to Government, 36; information on historical materials in *Annual Reports* of, 44; general index to *Reports* of, 44.

American Historical Review, 14.

American Library Annual, 30.

American State Papers, 35, 38.

Ames, John G., *Comprehensive Index*, 37.

Angle, Paul M., criticism of the Minor Collection of Lincoln Letters, 66 n.

Annual American Catalogue, 27.

Annual Library Index, 29.

Annual Literary Index, 25, 29.

Annual Magazine Subject-Index, 31.

Appendices, use of in historical monograph, 132.

Arabian Nights, 99.

Archæologia Americana, 61 n.

Archer, Gabriel, 60 *et seq.*

Archives, guides to a. of United States and foreign governments, 38–39; of states, 45.

Arnold, Benedict, 133.

Authorship, determination of, 60 *et seq.*, 97.

Autobiographies, as historical sources, 87–88.

Auxiliary sciences, xii.

"Background" courses, 1.

Bancroft, George, method of note-taking, 51; authorship of Johnson's presidential messages, 64; patriotic bias, 91–92; *History of the United States*, 92, 95; literary distortion, 95.

Bancroft Library, resources of, 6.

Bassett, John Spencer, *Short History*, 105.

Beale, Howard K., on diary of Gideon Welles, 71 and n.; *Critical Year*, 89 n.

Beecher, Henry Ward, as disseminator of slander, 89.

Bibliography, preparation of working b., 7–45; use of dictionary catalogue, 7–10; forms for notes on, 10; appraisal of books, 10, 11, 13, 14; essential data in b., 11–12; sample forms for, 12–13; filing notes on, 14–15; use of books in compiling, 15–16; forms for listing references to periodicals, etc., 17–18; items from footnotes, 20–22; references to government documents, 21–22; bibliographies in comprehensive histories, 23–24; how to find existing bibliographies, 24–25; use of general catalogues of books, 25–28; use of

ADDENDA

P. 31. *Social Science Abstracts* was discontinued with the issue of December, 1932.

P. 38. To the references on this page relating to foreign affairs should be added Samuel Flagg Bemis and Grace Gardner Griffin, *Guide to the Diplomatic History of the United States, 1775–1921*. Government Printing Office, Washington, 1935.

P. 39. The *Handbook of Manuscripts* is supplemented by Dr. C. W. Garrison's "List of Manuscript Collections in the Library of Congress to July, 1931," in the American Historical Association *Annual Report* for 1930, volume I.

P. 40. *The Checklist of Collections of Personal Papers* is superseded by *Manuscripts in Public and Private Collections in the United States*, issued by the Superintendent of Documents in 1924.

P. 103. The tentative conclusion in the text is practically confirmed by a statement which Calhoun made in the Oregon debate. In this he admitted that he had favored the Missouri Compromise, but asserted that he had come to regard his former view as a great error. See Crallé, Richard K., *The Works of John C. Calhoun*, I, 372; III, 185; IV, 346. See also Thomas H. Benton, *Thirty Years View*, 139–141.